Praise for Export Proof
by Doug Frey

I0209469

"Export Proof" represents the only detailed reference I have seen outlining the very practical steps of all the details necessary to build, sustain, and sell a business. It's a great glossary for all the tools needed along the way. Way more than a handbook!"

DOUG OBERHELMAN,
Former CEO and Executive Chairman of Caterpillar, INC

"This book hit close to home for me. I am a self employed general contractor and I fully understand the leap you need to take to be a self employed business man. I relate to Doug's strong conviction and commitment towards employees, which has made his business so successful."

DAVE HINMAN, Custom home builder, California

"Frey's book is more than great guide for starting up or buying an export-proof business. It provides insight to running a business, inspiring a workforce, and building for success that will be valuable to leaders in any organization! Anyone seeking success in business or life will find it well worth their time to read Export Proof."

AMY BATSON, Chief Fundraising Officer, Ducks Unlimited

"Every business owner should read this book. It's made me reevaluate my business and make some long needed changes."

ROB GOKEY, Owner of Triple B Foods

"I have been in the service industry for thirty-five years as an electrical contractor. Doug's book hit square on the head with virtually all aspects of building a business. All of the formal education I received did not prepare me for life as a small business owner. If Export Proof would have been available 35 years ago, I am quite sure I could have avoided many of the high-cost mistakes I made, especially in the beginning.

I highly recommend anyone considering going into business or who may need a little help, to read Export Proof, and follow it step by step. In the end, their business life will be much easier and fulfilling."

RUSTY LEGG, President, Competitive Electric

"Great insight and tips for anyone starting or building a service business. Read this book and avoid the expensive mistakes that so many entrepreneurs make, especially in the beginning."

KEVIN RODGERS,
Founder & Former CEO, Delta Rigging & Tools

"Export Proof is a great handbook on the basics of business for anyone starting a business."

HALIE RICKETS, Owner of Dapper Hair in Austin, TX

"Doug Frey has provided a common sense, straightforward guide to making good decisions. He has also given wonderful advice on leadership that fits any situation common to great leaders.

Anyone thinking about starting a business or becoming a leader should have Export Proof in their briefcase and in the top drawer of their desk, for ready access."

DALE HALL, CEO, Ducks Unlimited

"Too often small business owners lose sight of the nuts and bolts of being a successful manager. Frey's real world experience is an excellent read for those wanting to run their own business."

TRACY YETT, Former Controller and CFO

"Export Proof is an easy read, packed full of great ideas."

COLE MOREHEAD, Owner and President, Xcel NDT

"Doug Frey has a proven track record of building successful businesses. Owners and operators can learn from his view of lawyers, accountants, and bankers. Doug has always been able to foster "partnerships" with these professionals, eliciting their expertise to his advantage."

DAVID BOUTIN, Market President, Frost Bank

"I have always admired Doug Frey's approach to business and life. If I had this book when I started my roofing business, I could have avoided a lot of mistakes, especially in the beginning."

SHAWN DECENTO,
Owner, Lone Star Roofing, San Antonio, TX

"With our rapidly changing demographics and the continuing impact of the world-economy, Doug Frey's candid lessons for building a trade-based service business are relevant, applicable and accurate!"

DAN THIEL, Chief Operating Officer, Wetlands America Trust

"Export Proof is a fantastic guide for anyone considering buying or building a trade based service business. I appreciate the use of the summary of key elements and terms at the end of each chapter."

STEVE BENSON, Retired Senior Executive

"I helped Doug take the leap and start his first business. But this book helped me evaluate my company exit strategies and prepare it for sustainability."

SCOTT RUPARD, Owner, Katy Steel

Export Proof

EXPORT

*How to Buy or Build
a Trade-Based
Service Business
and Create Local Jobs*

PROOF

DOUG FREY

CRANE
RIVER
PRESS

Crane River Press
Austin, TX

Published by
Crane River Press
Austin, TX

Library of Congress Control Number 2018952977

ISBN 978-0-9995306-1-0

Managing Editor: Mackenzie Smith
Copy Editors: Joshua Bennet Winer and Dylan Owens
Illustrations by Stacy Antoville
Book and Cover Design by Jason Kelley

Printed and bound in the U.S.A.
First Edition

Dedicated to my father

Contents

Foreword

Corey and I had just finished a tour of a commercial glass installation company I was looking to buy. Corey, my son-in-law, was full of questions he'd been dying to ask since he met me. He had a front-row seat to the payoff for building a thriving business — flexible hours, month-long vacations, a recliner and a big screen TV in my office. Corey wanted to know how a business owner could make it all work. At the time, he had a good job with one of the best companies in town. But, Corey was a quarterback in college: He wanted to be calling the plays of the business, not sitting on the bench. I had just signed the papers to sell the majority share of my oilfield service company to a private equity firm; the sale was a home run by any measure. I would be out of a job, but I enjoyed the business of business too much to sit on the back porch for the rest of my days.

I was looking to buy another company that could be built into something significant. I had no doubt the lessons I learned running the oilfield service company could be applied to other service businesses. The idea that I could coach while he quarterbacked our company made perfect sense. This book is a product of the discussions Corey and I have had since deciding to buy and grow a business together. I hope you find the information in it as valuable as Corey has with our commercial glass installation company.

A commercial glass and glazing company is a classic example of an export-proof business. It requires trained and trusted employees to perform a highly specialized, on-site service. A general contractor is never going to call a 1-800 number or import pre-made walls to have windows installed in their building. You need boots on the ground for this job. Construction projects will always need a service like ours. While many jobs in America have been lost to companies outsourcing work to other countries, service businesses that require skilled workers to do the work on-site are **export-proof.** Aside from being highly profitable, buying or building a trade-based service business provides the owner with the opportunity to build an environment for a "work family" to grow and thrive, which has been one of my greatest joys as a successful entrepreneur.

For Corey, the concept of creating export-proof businesses and jobs strikes a deep emotional chord. As a teenager living in a small town in Ohio, he witnessed foreign competition take over the local steel mill — by far the largest employer and economic driver in the community. Both his dad and his grandfather worked at the mill their whole lives. His friends expected to work there and live out their lives down the street from their families. When the mill came under new ownership, many of his dad's work friends were forced into retirement or laid off. The idea of working for significant pensions disappeared. For the first time in generations, adult children had to leave the community to seek employment. The change was devastating. Considering my success and Corey's hometown history, export-proof businesses are still viable enterprises to pursue in America.

Introduction

The box sat on my desk ready to be carried out the door. So this is how more than 20 years with the same company ends? No retirement party, no well-wishers — just colleagues avoiding eye contact. I felt like the walking dead carrying that box to my car. Like a lot of folks in the late '90s working in the oil industry, I had been laid off. With three kids getting ready to go to college it would be tough, near impossible, to "hunker down" and wait for a possible recovery.

My wife brought it up, saying, "With oil below $10 a barrel, no one is hiring, no matter how good you are. I trust your judgement more than any of the executives you've worked for. Why not consider running your own business?" In nearly 40 years of marriage, the only other words she's said that have held more meaning are "I do."

I t was 1999 and I was 44. I had been laid off from my job of 20-plus years. My wife, Allison, and I had seen it coming for some time. The oil industry had been in steady decline since prices had peaked in 1981. Watching other people get laid off was a regular occurrence during my career at Amoco. I figured, statistically, it was just a matter of time before there was no chair for me when the music stopped. Several of my friends were running very successful trade-based service businesses (roofing, rebar installation, portable toilet rental). I wanted a lifestyle like theirs: boats, beach houses and lots of time for family and hobbies. Not knowing a thing about running a small business, I began pestering my friends with questions. I have included many of the lessons I learned from them in this book.

During my early investigations into owning a business it became apparent to me that the real opportunities were available in trade-based service businesses — jobs and work that couldn't be exported or done somewhere else. One of the calls I made soon after being laid off was to a former business associate and friend of 20 years. He knew of a business for sale in West Texas, but didn't have time to evaluate it. I had nothing but time, so I headed to Odessa to check it out. Desert X-Ray was an oilfield service company that inspected the welds on pipelines and pressure vessels. Their sales were under a million a year.

Not long after my first visit to assess the business, I decided to take the leap. My former business associate became my partner and we struck a deal, buying the assets of Desert X-Ray. We closed on July 8, 1999. Fifteen years later to the day, we sold Desert to a public company. It had grown to over 500 employees and over $100 million in annual sales.

This book is my story, and a handbook for buying and building a successful export-proof service business.

The Secret Sauce

During the 15 years I spent building a trade-based business, I made enough mistakes-turned-learning-opportunities to earn a self-proclaimed MBCA: my Master's in Blue-Collar Administration is widely appreciated by friends, family and acquaintances who regularly seek my experience and expertise on the subject. I am glad to share both the mistakes and the successes that led me here today. From those 15 years of adventure and misadventure, I have distilled a functional recipe for running and growing a successful company.

"Secret sauce" is a term private equity folks and other business professionals often use to refer to the special or differentiating factor that results in some companies growing like crazy while others in the same industry struggle. Because of our success with Desert, I have been asked a thousand times: "What was the secret sauce at your company?" This book has the answers.

Our approach was evolutionary (okay, occasionally revolutionary) and felt like a natural progression — the "right" way to move forward based on our mission and common values. The combination of how things worked together, along with the great employees at Desert, made up our "secret sauce."

Many management styles are effective and none are perfect. Much of my advice will work just as well for managing people in big companies as it does for those in small ones. Corey's style at the glass company is quite different from mine. His success is a testament that the principles presented in this book can work with a wide variety of people and styles to create your own secret sauce for success.

By doing the things I enjoyed the most and delegating the rest, I ended up working *on* the business instead of *in* it. Almost by accident, this turned out to be a key component to growing Desert.

I have found that a lot of "how-to" business books are written for the white-collar, college educated crowd, and don't always translate to trade-based service businesses very well. This book is an example, an important lesson that for many products and nearly all service businesses: the differentiating factor lies in how the product — information in this case — is delivered.

With no fancy MBA, I learned accounting and business skills the hard, expensive way. I said before that I quizzed my friends who owned businesses, but I also approached people I admired with questions about what made them successful. From a deli owner to one of the largest corporations in the world, I have listened, watched and learned from the best.

As a young engineer, I often joked about people who went with their gut, preferred hard data analysis rather than a gut feeling. But, over the years I saw great leaders of companies making decisions that used data for guidelines, but they were not bound by only what could be measured or listed, especially when those decisions involved people. Now, I have found that the subconscious can often take more into account than the smartest person could list, much less quantify. This fact, plus knowing it was my company and I could live with the result of my decision, ended up with me often just doing what seemed right at the time. Working in a big company, too often I had to live with a decision that someone else had made, like laying off my friends.

This book is a compilation of business ideas and processes that were the result of doing what I thought was right as the owner of a small business. One of the greatest things about owning a business is you have the freedom to do things your way, the way you think and feel is right — particularly how you treat people, employees, customers and others. It can be extremely rewarding financially as well as emotionally. I wrote this book as a way to help others pursue and live their dream of owning a successful business.

1

Taking the Leap

I once saw a great presentation on "what keeps you from owning your own business." The key point was a picture of a paycheck. Yup, the security of a steady paycheck keeps most people from following their dreams. This is despite the fact that most millionaires own their own businesses, well-documented in the book, "The Millionaire Next Door: The Surprising Secrets of America's Wealth," by Thomas Stanley and William Danko.

I graduated from college in 1977 with a bachelor's degree in mechanical engineering. Upon graduation, I began a career with Amoco, the oil exploration and production division of Standard Oil Indiana, the fifth largest corporation in the world at the time. It seemed like everyone thought that if you went to work for a major company and didn't totally screw up, you would be employed with them until you retired. In 1998, BP bought Amoco and in 1999, they decided I no longer needed a steady paycheck.

As a result, this book is a guide for those looking to go into business for themselves, and a reminder that there is life after layoff.

A few years before I was laid off, I started having more thoughtful conversations about owning a business with friends who had their own. I continue to have those discussions on a regular basis. It is a good practice to cultivate friends with similar goals. The ability to discuss mutual problems makes them a lot less intimidating. Several minds working on a problem will almost always come up with a better solution. Even better if you can find someone who has been down the road you are going and is willing to be a mentor.

Losing my job at Amoco always seemed like a possibility. My wife, Allison, and I both knew it would take money to start a business. So, we lived frugally and saved like crazy! For over a decade we used an old door on sawhorses as our dining room table. It was definitely out of place in our suburban neighborhood. We took plenty of ribbing from our friends for it, though I often pointed out that the table was never off-putting enough that they would turn down a meal at our house. Like Warren Buffett (the other guy from Nebraska), I believed in the future of this country and investing in it through the stock market.

Good fortune and timing were also with us. The 1980s and '90s were a time of tremendous returns in the stock market. We put the money we could have invested in dining room furniture into Microsoft, a little-known tech company in the 1980s. You can guess how that turned out. I always say, "It's good to have options." Our savings and return on investments in the '80s gave us great comfort and made it possible for me to consider buying a business when I was eventually laid off.

Life After Layoff

Whether or not you have actually been laid off, there is a lot you can do in preparation if you are considering starting or buying a business. Seek out and ask for the advice of those who are currently in business, especially successful ones. Don't be afraid to ask for help; few people turn down a sincere request for it. If you're lucky, you will find someone who wants to help. Make an effort to nurture advisors into mentors for ongoing support.

"What do you want to do for a living?" The answer to this question is complicated. It really means: Where do you want to live? How much income do you want/need? What kind of work do you enjoy? Inside? Outside? With people or by yourself? With computers or definitely not with computers? You get the idea. Then you have to consider your spouse, girlfriend, boyfriend, kids, parents, health care, cost of living, your commute and on and on. If you are thinking of starting your own business, start with determining your strengths and identifying where you need help.

The "Blue-Collar" Opportunity

Being a Scoutmaster was one of the most satisfying things I have ever done. The ability to influence young men during a difficult transition in their lives was very rewarding, especially since it was a transformational time for myself as well. During one of our campfire discussions, one of the dads said something about his son learning a trade, like being an electrician or plumber instead of going to college. In that circle, such talk was heresy. Didn't everyone want their kids to go to college? He went on to explain that manufacturing work in the U.S. had been in decline as those jobs were shipped overseas. Stateside, computers were taking the place of many clerical positions, leaving relatively low-paying service jobs as employment options. On the bright side, trade-based service businesses were still offering high-paying jobs, as he pointed out: "You are not going to ship your clogged toilet overseas to get fixed." It made me think about the necessity of these types of trades and their future in our country.

Trade businesses = export-proof

My friend's comment on not outsourcing trade jobs made a lot of sense. I wanted to own a business with good growth potential; a business that would never dissipate from lack of necessity, regardless of advances in technology. I was interested in working with people to grow careers by providing them with opportunities to learn more about their trade. And I wanted to make money. So, when I started looking for businesses to buy, I had my eyes out for a trade-based service business.

Export-proof businesses involve a hands-on skill; one that can be learned on the job or at a trade school. Our success at Desert X-Ray as an oilfield service company is a specific example of a trade-based business. However, the category in general is very broad. It includes nearly every construction trade: plumbing, electrician, automation, glass/window installation, painting, framing, foundation setting, roofing, flooring (tile, carpet, wood) installation, drywall, pool building, landscaping, mowing, sprinkler installation and repair and computer hardware installation and repair. Moving, trucking, cleaning, pet training, pet grooming, pet walking, pet daycare, pet kennel, nail salon, hair salon, power washing and carwashes are also included; and these are just ones my wife has used in the last month.

Once you decide which type of business to start, you will need to begin deciding how the company will be organized. This involves your role as owner and hiring the right team to complement your vision for the business.

The Work Myth

It's a commonly held belief that people who own a business are chained to their work 24/7. To some extent, that's true. The owner who can't trust well-trained employees to do their job can easily fall into the habit of using all their time and energy managing every detail. The boss who can't commit to something being done, who changes things endlessly (or has their staff change things), might be known as a workaholic or a perfectionist, but they will also be known as the one who is working around the clock, micromanaging. Having faith in your team and knowing when enough is enough will cut down on the owner's time working *in* the business, allowing more time to work *on* it.

To my employees, it was a sign of accomplishment that I trusted them enough to do their jobs without me around telling them what to do. Hiring staff that are better than you or that complement your abilities may be the most important step to the growth of your company and personal freedom.

Many small businesses are unable to grow beyond the point where everything, including daily operations, are dependent on the owner. The perception that most business owners work long hours is a true one. I had a different vision, based on what I saw from my friends who were business owners. After I was laid off, it dawned on me that several of my mentors who ran successful small businesses had more time to golf, fish and hunt than any corporate executive I knew. This book should serve as a roadmap to guide you beyond building a small company reliant on the owner to a sustainable one with daily operations independent of the owner.

You Are Not Alone

Starting or running your own business will impact everyone in your family. So if you have a spouse or partner, make sure you have their support before taking the leap. Luckily, in my case, my wife supported and encouraged my ventures. We were able to assess the learning curve together and discuss all the risks, rewards, pros and cons (especially the money) involved with owning a business. It's a great asset to have someone you trust looking things over and pointing out something you may have otherwise missed. If you have children, it will impact your ability to participate in their activities and affect time spent with your extended family. Holidays are often busy and everyone wants time off, which can leave the owner running things. If you try to run your business without the support of your spouse or partner, you will more than likely end up with the company going under, getting a divorce or both. Having a shared understanding of the risks involved and what it will take to be prosperous is imperative.

Picking a Partner

In my case, my partner provided critical knowledge that complemented my own; he had experience running a success-ful oilfield service company. My expertise was in processes and procedures that made big companies work. The combination allowed us to grow from a mom and pop service company to a regional, and then eventually national, business. Think about what skills, talents or resources your partner will bring. You will have a formal, legal partnership, so it's important to share the same values.

Not all partnerships are built with equal investments. One common arrangement involves one person providing the capital (sometimes called a "silent partner") and the other providing the knowledge, or **sweat equity,** to run the business. It's complicated — have a good lawyer guide you through the agreement.

Partnering can be challenging even during the good times. Success can create greed. Many good partnerships have broken up over dividing the spoils of success. Maintaining a good relationship in tough times is difficult, especially if your vision and level of commitment don't line up. A business breakup can be as emotionally and financially devastating as a divorce; choose your partner carefully.

Fear of the unknown keeps many people from starting or buying a business. There are plenty of scary stories out there, and some of them are true. Many small businesses go under after a short time. This book should remove some of that fear, prevent you from making common mistakes, and open the door to owning a business.

Definitions and Key Ideas

- **Export-proof business:** a trade-based service business consisting of jobs that can't be outsourced because they require people to be physically present to provide services to other people or businesses.

- **Secret sauce:** the term business professionals often use to refer to the special or differentiating factor that separates the companies that grow like crazy from those in the same industry that are average.

- **Sweat equity:** equity earned in a business or enterprise from the investment of time and effort. (Most equity is acquired with a capital investment.)

Definitions and Key Ideas (continued)

- **Trade-based service business:** businesses that involve a hands-on skill that can be learned on the job or at a trade school.

- Make an effort to nurture advisors into mentors for ongoing support.

- The security of a steady paycheck keeps most people from following their dreams.

- You are not alone! Think about who you can count on for advice, and also who will be affected by your decision to start or buy a business.

- Figure out how you can eventually work on the business, not just in it.

- Hiring staff that are better than you or that complement your abilities may be the most important step to the growth of your company and personal freedom.

- Picking a business partner is one of the most important decisions you will make in this journey. Choose well.

2

Stages of a Company

After watching some companies constantly struggle while others thrived, I categorized small businesses into three stages of development. This chapter defines Stages One, Two and Three so you can identify which stage your company is in and manage how and when to advance to the next one.

Stage One is working *in* the company; Stage Two is working *on* the company; and Stage Three is oversight of the company. Growth is driven by hiring the right people at the right time to maximize **organizational capability — the ability of a group to get things done**. As you move through the stages, revenue and net income should increase dramatically. Understanding where you are now and knowing where you want to go is part of the building process.

Stage One is what most people associate with owning a business. I call it the "you *are* the company" stage. From unlocking the door in the morning to closing the shop at night, nothing happens without the involvement and oversight of the owner. Most trade-based companies are very small, made up of just one or two crews and sometimes referred to as a "Chuck and a truck" business. Few grow to a significant size. Many service businesses start out as sole proprietors, with the owner providing a skilled service. They might eventually grow enough to hire other technicians providing similar services and a bookkeeper to handle the overflow of paperwork.

Consider Stage One a startup phase. Some businesses never get beyond hiring technicians and a bookkeeper to handle increasing customers. This may work for you, but take into consideration how hard it will be to leave your work (vacation, weekends, holidays, etc.) if it falls on your shoulders to keep things afloat. Stage One does offer flexibility, meaning you decide what tasks you take on and when to work, but profit is typically a function of the owner's personal effort. That means even though you have the flexibility to manage how much work you take on, if you aren't working or dispatching the work to someone else, no one is getting paid. Many trade-based businesses stuck in Stage One struggle to grow past just a few technicians because the owner is unwilling to step back and rely on the people he or she hired to take on the work needed to grow the company.

Some types of small businesses are dependent on the talent or skills of a particular person, like interior decorators, custom cabinetmakers or chef-owned restaurants. They are inherently small, with little growth potential or small profit margins. These businesses are often small by choice. The principle owner is able to maintain control over the product by making it themselves or personally overseeing the process. Other businesses may have great *potential* for growth and profit, but everything still depends on the owner, by choice. If your business is small or low in profit, you will end up with a full-time job for yourself and not much more — a perfectly acceptable outcome for some folks. Trade-based businesses are **scalable, which means they have the ability to grow much bigger if the owner first hires folks who provide services, and second, builds organizational capability that supports a larger enterprise.**

Plumbers, electricians, landscapers, oilfield service workers, welders, mechanics, construction workers — **these are examples of businesses that often stay small, but have the potential to scale up if the owner commits to pushing the business beyond Stage One.**

Maybe you have no desire to grow your business beyond personal effort and a small support team. I suggest you still do some simple analysis to work *on* the business. What is your ideal salary or income? This can be determined by looking at the principal item or service you sell and the profit on each item. Understanding profit on what you sell is important to know and is not easy to track when you are selling a service and hours are your core product. Consider a plumber. There is the cost to get to your house with the proper equipment, insurance, gas and travel time. Do they have to do any prep work prior to providing the service? Don't forget medical and liability insurance, payroll and income taxes! Money required includes tools and an inventory of frequently used parts. And all businesses have "back-office" work after the service call: sending an invoice, collecting, depositing/banking, paying their own bills, rent, utilities, office space, etc. Be sure to include all of these costs in your rate.

Once you understand your product cost, then you can start determining the price you have to charge to make a profit. But can you sell it for that much or even more? What is the market? How much do your competitors charge? Next you need to determine how many of those items or services have to be sold to generate the income or salary you want. What does it take to sell this many (more people, equipment, etc.)? Do not leave this analysis for your spare time or "someday." It is your job as CEO (even if you are the only employee) to know these things. Use this analysis to get where you want to go:

IDEAL SALARY =
(NUMBER OF ITEMS SOLD X PRICE OF EACH) - ALL EXPENSES

Many small businesses fail because the owner never fully understands the total cost of the product. Working harder and selling more is not the solution to that problem.

Stage Two is the point where you start hiring folks to help you run the business. It requires you to commit to work *on* the company. Your commitment will take you out of the role of personally providing services and dispatching jobs to focusing on work processes necessary for evolving into an organization that operates without you. You will need to find employees with complementary skills and then work to empower, train and trust them to do their jobs (read more on how to do that in the chapter on "Managing Managers"). This all sounds very exciting, but Stage Two is the place where you'll experience the lion's share of growing pains associated with expansion. Finding the right people is never easy. Assume your new role will mean learning skills you may not be familiar with yet. Everyone (customers, employees, partners) will still come to you with everything. In addition to all that, in order to bring in more people to complement your skill set, you will need to consider how to pay for those hires. It's a tough call. Do you take on the expense of hiring folks and hope the company grows so you can afford to pay them? Or do you add sales and services, risking overloading staff and providing poor service so you can afford to hire more employees? This conundrum is a never-ending balancing act between profit and expenses. One way to pay for those new hires is by taking out a **line of credit**, or an **LOC**. It is a common move for businesses who want to grow and increase profit potential by building a team to run the company.

When we bought Desert in 1999, it was a business in late Stage One or early Stage Two. The owner was still involved in daily operations. His wife was doing the bookkeeping. Besides the operations manager, the only other administrative staff was the receptionist. After the sale, we had to hire a bookkeeper to replace the previous owner's wife. The owner had trained service technicians to handle additional work, but he had no plan for growth. Desert was somewhere in limbo, possibly the worst place to be in the Stages of Development. Once you start employing other people, their livelihood is in your hands. If you don't have a plan to grow, making decisions on a daily basis will be very difficult. This is because your reasoning isn't based on an end-goal, but on what you think is best for the week or month ahead with no plan for the fiscal year, let alone the years to come.

A bookkeeper is a good start. But to up your game in Stage Two, you will need someone who can work *on* the business. As company profits grow, invest in hiring a degreed accountant who can manage a small staff to handle accounts payable, invoicing, payroll, bank compliance, insurance and benefits. This is an expensive but important step. As the company grows you will eventually need a controller who can design financial performance metrics, select an enterprise software system and oversee its installation. The controller will also analyze financial and operating performance data. If your company gets big enough to start buying other similar companies or to become a public company, you will need a Chief Financial Officer (CFO).

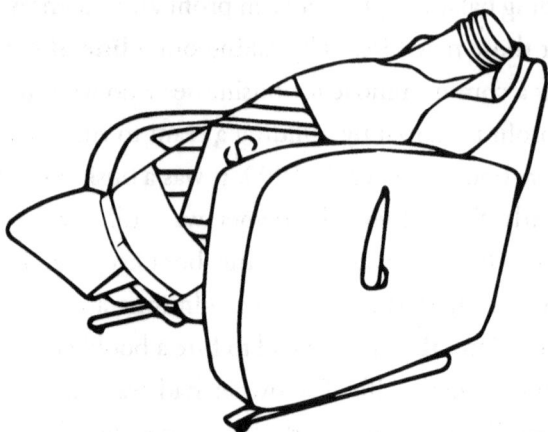

One day, after a few good years of growth at Desert, my business partner had a fancy recliner delivered to the office. As we admired it together, he pointed at the recliner and said, "I want you to spend more time in that chair and less time in that chair," pointing to the one behind my desk. "You make ten times more money when you work on the company than you do working in the company."

Building a plan and a team are at the heart of what it takes to really expand. This work is tedious. Stage Two involves the financial risk and problems associated with hiring employees. But working *on* the business is where the big money is made in the long run. It can eventually lead to a company that can operate without the owner.

When we bought the glass installation company, it was clearly in Stage One. No project got done without the owner being involved. By hiring an office manager/bookkeeper, project manager, a few administrative staff and promoting some field hands to crew leads, the glass company is now in early Stage Two. Corey is still doing a significant amount of actual work in the company, but he has built enough organizational capability with other positions that a lot gets done without him. The majority of his day is still spent working in the business, not on it. When he gets to the point where he is working on the business, he'll spend more time hiring and developing people than working directly on projects.

With Corey's hard work and my coaching, the company has already grown revenues significantly compared to when we started. Even more exciting to me is our plan to hire more project managers and promote some folks, so Corey can spend more time with my grandchildren and the company can grow substantially more. It's good to have a plan!

Stage Three is when the company can run on autopilot. In this stage, most critical functions are not dependent on you, which means you will be rewarded with more personal freedom than you were in Stages One and Two. Once you reach Stage Three, your company will be sustainable, positioned to last for many years, if not generations. Sustainable businesses do not require the owner to be present for everyday operations because the organizational capability of the company is strong enough to operate on its own. Sales and marketing efforts are constantly renewing demand for the service you are providing. Of course, services provided are always changing in response to the market. But you won't have to worry about the business being undercut by a cheaper labor force in a foreign country. That's the beauty of owning an export-proof business.

> *In 1950, a teenage construction worker in Detroit made the decision to pass on a college scholarship so he could start building houses. By the mid-1990s, he had turned the company into a giant, with offices in 25 states. William J. Pulte insisted all employees call him "Bill." PulteGroup is one of the largest homebuilders in the United States. From the beginning, he hired folks to do what it took to grow a company so he could focus on what he knew best — the actual construction. He was known as a hands-on leader, and traveled extensively to building sites to examine the quality of work and construction processes, regularly making changes and improvements for his customers. Pulte was still climbing ladders on job sites into his 70s. His story is a good example of how you need to work in the business to*

know what your company does and how it is done, but
it also proves that he knew he couldn't do everything to
grow the business by himself.

Stage Three businesses are the most attractive to buyers because the company is self-sufficient. That's why building a company to sell is a common goal for many businesses. But aiming for sustainability is just as important if you are planning to keep it all in the family. Some companies see the value of having family members involved for generations as one of the principal benefits of their business model. The founder often becomes the chairman or coach while newer family members apprentice. This approach allows family members to work and contribute their particular strengths to the organization.

What keeps business owners from moving through the Stages and ultimately achieving sustainability? Well, you have to know about the Stages to understand how to move through them, so if you are reading this you are on the right track. Knowing what you want and planning how to get there will help you achieve your goals. Building organizational capability is a big part of what it takes to grow in Stage Two and Three. But even when you plan, you can still run into problems. For many owners, "busywork" — i.e., emails, long meetings with no defined objectives, phone calls and generally just keeping things running — can be hard to walk away from. Busywork is endless and does not allow time for you to work *on* the company. Stay focused on the important stuff.

Starting with the end in mind is critical, especially in the planning process. Regardless of what stage your company is in today, think about where you would like to be one year, five years, ten years from now. Do you still want to be running everything yourself and allowing profit to be directly tied to your availability? Would you like to have the option to eventually sell your business? Or would you like to be the CEO of a company that can run itself seamlessly when you decide to take a long vacation? There is no right answer. But considering these questions will help you plan for growth, and understanding the Stages will serve as a guide for advancing to the next one.

Building an Organization

Stage Two and Three involve building organizational capacity.

The highest level of organizational capacity exists when your business is able to run without your involvement. To get there, you must have well-developed internal processes, rules and expectations that clearly state how different situations are handled. Each employee should understand the company's vision and how their role within the company will help achieve it.

It's all about people, people, people.

The first steps to building organizational capacity at any stage are making sure your employees have the tools, training and information they need to do their current job, as well as the opportunities to train for their next one.

The key to successful transition between the Three Stages of growth is building sustainable organizational capacity.

Over the years, I have looked at a wide range of companies to buy as additions to an existing company or as investments.

In several cases, the owner held on too tight, keeping their company permanently stuck in Stage One. Often, they had already started winding the company down, reducing size and clientele to maintain a manageable level as they worked less and less in the business. When the owners were finally ready to let go and sell the company in their old age, they only had a few customers left. The customers that remained were personally loyal to the owner, and therefore unlikely to stay on under new ownership. They really had nothing left to sell except some worn-out equipment and a shortlist of customers loyal to the owner. Dreams of a big payday never materialized. If you decide to remain in Stage One with everything dependent on you, there won't be much of a company to sell at the end as an exit strategy.

Understanding the importance of organizational capability and identifying where your business stands among the Stages of Development will serve as the framework for a strong business model. The next section explains how to put it all into writing, and who you can count on to help along the way. Read on!

Definitions and Key Ideas

- **Capital costs:** the money it takes to buy all the tools, equipment, parts, inventory and other stuff it takes to run a business.

- **Line of credit (LOC):** an amount of credit extended to a borrower usually secured by accounts receivable (existing sales). *Read more on the process of taking out an LOC in Chapter 8.*

- **Organizational capability:** a group's ability (through skills process and people) to get things done.

Definitions and Key Ideas (continued)

- **Scalability:** the ability to grow by providing more of the same service. For example, expanding by hiring more techs and support staff, or opening additional offices that provide the same service.

- **Stage One:** the startup phase; it requires the work of the owner to get almost anything done.

- **Stage Two:** the fast-growing phase; it requires the owner to work on the business and to hire the right folks. Growth is no longer limited by the time and talents of the owner.

- **Stage Three:** business is sustainable; it doesn't require the owner to be present for everyday operations because the organizational capability of the company is strong enough to operate on its own.

- Aim for sustainability.

- Busywork is endless and does not allow time for you to work on the company.

- Start with the end in mind.

- Building organizational capacity is the key to transitioning successfully between the Three Stages of growth.

3

Building a Business

Now that you've decided to grow your business through the Stages; let's talk about how to get there. A plan is important if you are starting to think about buying a business, critical if you are in that long, second stage of growing your business; and key for maintaining sustainability in Stage Three. But even basic business stuff covered in the next few chapters can be overwhelming, especially if you are already running a company. Read through it, absorb what you can, then come back to this chapter and use it as a guide when you are ready to start drawing up a business plan.

Speaking of guides, this chapter also highlights the importance of building a team of professionals that will be indispensable to you as a business owner. It is ideal to have a plan before you start, and to have that team working for you from the get-go. But don't beat yourself up if you aren't there yet. If you want to make it to the next stage, it is a considerable process to get there.

Planning

The basis of a business plan is a spreadsheet with estimated future cash flows for both income and expenses. In addition to the numbers, you need to explain your ideas for the future. This will include marketing, sales efforts, increased productivity and expansion, among other tactics. If you are purchasing an existing business, you will need to investigate and understand the accounting for recent historical revenues and expenditures, which I discuss at length in Chapter 9.

This information should be kept in a spreadsheet with revenues at the top, followed by expenses associated with generating said revenues. Overhead expenses such as rent, utilities and insurance go below that. Don't forget payroll taxes! If you've never "made payroll" before, you may be surprised at how much tax the employer pays on behalf of an employee. Plan for it so it won't come as a shock! Finally — profit — your bottom line, is generated by subtracting the expenses from the revenue.

A business plan is essentially a profit and loss statement over an extended period of time. So get your hands on a P&L statement of a similar business — it will be invaluable. You will find categories of expenses and revenues, which are a great starting point for building your own business plan. It's impossible to dream up all the categories of expenses to plan for if you start from scratch. These little items will eat up all your profits, so missing small things can cause big financial problems.

I have friends who have researched businesses similar to their own by hanging around to count employees and customers, guessing their salaries and purchases. Some have even worked in a similar business to get hands-on experience and better understand what they were getting into. Taking the time to dig in deep here can save you from going bust and ensure you are entering a big decision with your eyes wide open. Anything you can do to understand revenue and expenses before you go all-in is worth the effort.

In addition to a spreadsheet that covers the cash requirements for running and growing a business, you need to have a plan that identifies the organizational requirements that match your financial business plan. These include: the type and number of employees, the organizational departments, and the time required to execute your financial plan. They should all be streamlined in a cohesive, overall plan. Make sure you are accounting for the people you will need to employ now and in the future.

The Whole Enchilada

I was sitting in the audience at the annual luncheon held by the Odessa Chamber of Commerce when they announced the Entrepreneur of the Year. The winner was all smiles as she stepped forward to receive her award. As a regular in her restaurant, I often saw her working wherever an extra pair of hands were needed. She could be seen seating customers, delivering orders to each table, chatting with patrons about their meal, closing out their checks and thanking them for their business. She mentioned sales reaching one million dollars during her acceptance speech. How many plates of $6.99 cheese enchiladas (their specialty) did she have to sell per day to reach a million dollars in revenue?

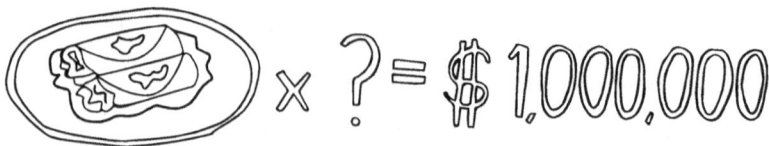

This type of analysis is good to use as a building block for your business plan. What is the core product you are selling? What will it cost to make and how many will you sell in a day, a week, a month, a year? What about the second year? Then, you need to factor in the expenses associated with making that item: labor, materials, a space to make it and sell it, electricity, air conditioning — you get the picture. It will take considerable effort to achieve "good" numbers. Rent, utilities, insurance and other overhead expenses that can be determined in advance should be assessed accurately. Make sure you are realistic in your expectations of sales. Assess the numbers monthly for the first two years and annually after that. If you don't have much spare operating capital, then you might want to do a daily analysis for the first 90 days, since it is likely you will be burning cash throughout this time. The first day you turn a profit, a celebration is in order. That goes for the first week, month —and double for the first year!

PROFIT = SALES (REVENUE) - EXPENSES

Warning: Profit on Paper is not Cash on Hand

Running out of operating cash is a common cause of failure for small businesses, so build a cash flow statement in addition to the business plan. You can run out of money even if your business is profitable on day one. How is that possible? It's simple, in many businesses you sell things or provide services. Then, you bill the customer, who might take 30-90 days to pay. This situation is common among service businesses. If you don't have enough cash to keep things running until you get paid, you can go out of business — even though you were theoretically profitable on day one. Most businesses have to pay for equipment, supplies, products and labor up front, getting paid *after* making the sale. The money required to operate the business (rent, salaries, insurance, supplies, etc.) until revenue from sales comes in is called **working capital**. Service companies, especially growing ones, also need capital for new equipment, trucks and such. These are referred to as **CapEx requirements**. Be sure to include both in your business plan.

Sure, some businesses get paid with a credit card as soon as a sale is made. But they still have to spend up front on materials, inventory and labor. Additionally, for credit card sales, they will pay 3-10 percent to the card company for managing the transaction. In many businesses, that is most of the profit. Accountants use a cash flow statement to track actual cash in and out of the business on a daily, weekly and monthly basis. A cash flow statement records sales and expenses as the cash is actually spent or collected. It tracks the items (expense and revenues) necessary to make sure that capital/savings, plus cash coming in, is sufficient to cover cash going out for long enough to keep the business open. It is similar to a profit and loss statement, but does not have non-cash items such as depreciation or **amortization**. It also does not accrue sales or expenses. Understanding the cash needs of your business is critical.

Not all sales are created equal. In some sales, you might get paid immediately; in others, the customer's money might take a month to come through. **The time between when the service is provided and when payment is made controls how much working capital you will need to keep the business running.**

There are standard accounting methods to recognize this difference in sales (revenue). Recognizing sales when you actually get paid is called **cash basis accounting**; recognizing a sale when it is earned (i.e. when the service has been provided but not yet paid for) is called **accrual basis accounting.** The Internal Revenue Service lets you choose which you want to use for tax purposes. Most small businesses choose cash basis tax accounting because it allows you to pay taxes after you have the money in hand. Accrual basis tax accounting requires you to pay taxes on "sales" that you have not been paid for yet, which can create a trap for business owners unaware of this effect on taxes.

You will need to use a spreadsheet to build your business plan and cash flow statement. Don't try to make them from scratch! There are many software and book solutions commercially available to help you build your first business plan. Look for one that fits your style and skill set. Use online guides or workbooks designed for building business plans.

I suggest that **after building the first draft of your business plan, cut sales in half and double expenses.** Sales come slow and there will always be unexpected expenses, so be a harsh judge when it comes to predicting these two important elements of your plan. Business owners are usually and often necessarily optimistic — but don't let that creep into your business plan. It is better to deal with harsh reality in the planning stage than in real life.

Setting Prices

With physical products, it's easier to set prices based on the cost of parts and labor, adding overhead and profit. But how much profit? Certainly, you have to be competitive with similar products, but people pay more for quality. The same is true in the service world — people will pay more for high-quality service. So how much do you need to charge?

As a service company, we learned a good rule of thumb over the years: **charge three times the amount that labor costs to make a decent profit.** Here, "decent profit" meant enough to save money during the good times to keep the doors open through the bad ones. The long-term health of a business is critical to a long-term employment and stable career for everyone, not just the owner.

Reality Check

When we bought Desert X-Ray, I estimated reasonable predictions for sales growth and capital costs for equipment based on accounting data. Unfortunately, the oil patch did not rebound as fast as I had predicted (you have to be an optimist to buy a business, but be careful it doesn't color your forecasts) and the fleet of trucks did not have the life left in them shown on the depreciation table at the time of purchase. The trucks were junk. We had to replace them all in two years instead of the five I had planned for. What effect did this have? I seldom took home any pay the first three years. My family was still living back in Houston and I was commuting to Odessa every week. We were waiting to see if the company was going to make it before selling the house in Houston and moving the family to West Texas. With my oldest child in college and two in high school, the pressure was on to make the company successful. Retreat was not an option. This had to work, and I would move heaven and earth to make it happen. It was a good thing we had savings to live on, because we had little money coming into the family from the business for almost three years. I was glad to have the support of my wife, Allison, who often told me during this tough time that if anyone could make it work, I could.

For more than two years, I shared an 800-sq-ft house with John, a traveling salesman whose family was also back in Houston. We called it "Casa de Oro" because of the yellow Christmas lights left on all year. Casa de Oro was an incubator for a lot more than the chickens John kept in the backyard. Many of the ingredients in Desert's secret sauce were cooked up while rocking on the front porch. John went on to start several service companies and has been tremendously successful in his own right.

Casa de oro

One common reason for failure, or stunting the growth of a new business, is connected to the way the owner responds to perceived success. If the business is going well and the owner sees a lot of money coming into the company — which looks like a lot more than what they were making as an employee at another business — it may result in increased spending habits and an upward shift in lifestyle. This could include buying a fancy car or truck, a second home, a boat, going on an expensive vacation — money spent on personal luxuries that could be put back into the business. Owners might feel like they've made it or that they deserve it. But it's also possible that they have not set aside enough of the profits to form a safety net. You have to decide what you really want in the long term: a bigger business with longevity or a fancy lifestyle today. Maybe you want to own a perpetual Stage One business and you don't mind that your lifestyle, work commitment and financial stability are directly connected to the amount of work you do. In this case, take your profits and buy a boat or two. But if you are reading this and thinking that a boat isn't going to help you get to Stage Two or Three, you are thinking like someone who is looking ahead for many years. If you really want to grow, understand that **self-discipline in spending is required to win big in the long run.** A good friend of mine once said, "Sometimes you have to say no to what you want to say yes to what you *really* want."

Lawyers, Accountants and Bankers, OH MY!

Consider them your trusted advisors, there to help you build a framework for your business and keep it running within important legal and financial boundaries. Veering outside those boundaries leads to serious consequences, so consult with your team of professionals early on and throughout the process of running your business. These advisors may become good friends, so make sure you share your success with them, as they will be crucial when things get tough. You need them to answer when you call!

Lawyers

From the very beginning, hiring a lawyer is essential to the success of your business. Lawyers can help protect your assets by laying legal groundwork for what is and what isn't expected from you as an owner or a partner. Your lawyer will make sure you are registered to conduct business and lend advice on human resource issues. I worked more than 20 years for a major company and was never once involved in a lawsuit. It took less than six months owning my own business before I was involved in my first. Lawsuits can become a common occurrence, many with minimum merit, but must be responded to promptly. My wife will never forget the first time a policeman came to our front door with a subpoena for me. Be prepared!

Find a lawyer you are comfortable working with. Spend the necessary fee to interview them before hiring, making sure they have expertise in the area you will need them. Try to get a reference from someone you trust. Stick to using documents that *your* lawyer prepares. Each document contains a great deal of details, and you need a professional with your best interest in mind preparing and reviewing them. Sure, attorney fees are expensive, but allowing the other party's legal team to prepare the documents may end up costing you more in the long run.

Accountants

Accountants are necessary for taxes and keeping your bankers happy. A good accountant will help you structure your books so they yield useful data. What are your biggest expenses? What expenses give you key insight into growth? Midsize companies use multimillion-dollar enterprise software systems to yield financial reports. You can work with your accountant to get the small company equivalent.

The government is a lousy partner, taking their share up front and not giving you any help. Your accountant can advise you about tax rules. Discuss your plans so they can help you make good business decisions from an "after tax perspective." Rules are complex and constantly changing, so you need someone watching to make sure you don't overpay your "tax partner."

Your Second Set of Eyes

It's good practice to have a trusted CPA (Certified Public Accountant) do your income taxes and review your books every year. This is especially true in Stage One. You are often too busy running the business to pay attention to complex tax accounting requirements.

Knowing that, a lot of startups still skip this step because of the expense. This is a mistake. A second set of eyes looking at the business from a numbers perspective may see things someone running the day-to-day would miss. If you are buying a business, have your accountant review the financials provided, ask for a simple **quality of earnings analysis** and verify revenue. Pay a professional to look at the financial system in place. A CPA will help you apply a system of controls to prevent theft, or catch it before you do. They can also assess your risk of fraud and what you might need to change to prevent embezzlement. Trying to do all this yourself could be a very expensive lesson, one that makes paying for college look cheap. I know! Learn from my mistakes.

Either way, your bank will want a CPA report if you want to borrow any money. It is also comforting to partners, and everyone financially involved, to have an outsider go over the books. Additionally, if you ever decide to sell your business, having audited or other CPA-prepared financials will be required to get the best price.

Banker

Your banker is your friend, not an enemy! They may seem like a pain sometimes, but they are really trying to help you and keep the bank out of trouble at the same time. Your banker will be a key player in evaluating a company for purchase. They have experience with many different businesses and can point you in the right direction. Bankers can see things you missed or misunderstood in your analysis. Make an effort to have a senior or experienced banker assigned to your account. Sometimes I used the bank when I didn't necessarily need a loan, but wanted their expertise in evaluating a deal.

Bankers can also keep you flush with working capital, which is critical to growing a company. They can do this by setting you up with a line of credit, a flexible loan system. You can draw on it to purchase a business, buy the equipment needed to grow an existing business or cover operating expenses while you wait (what can seem like forever) for your customers to pay you.

New small business owners might be surprised to know that the **liquidity**, or cash availability, provided by bankers is almost always necessary because your "tax partner," the government, wants their share up front regardless of whether or not you are being paid or need capital for growth. Sometimes, startups look very successful until they have to pay taxes. Then, without liquidity, they go under.

It's in the bank's best interest to see you make a profit and to minimize your risks. Once, during a slow period at Desert, I felt like I had tried everything to boost sales, but it was slow for everyone in the oil patch. My banker called me up and suggested lunch. I suspected he wanted to check on things to see if he should be worried about their loan to us. He listened patiently for most of the meal while I explained what I had done to get sales and control costs. Toward the end of the meal, he leaned in and said, "Don't beat yourself up when things are bad, but don't think you're a genius when everyone's making big money, either!" When business was good, he would put me in my place by pointing out, "A rising tide lifts all boats." I would counter with, "A surfer rides the waves with grace and speed; a fishing bobber just goes up and down."

Insurance

Insurance is extremely complex. You need a smart, experienced agent to advise you on the risks that need to be insured. Requirements set by customers and the government should also be taken into consideration. Business involves risk and this decision is no different. Insurance will be one of your largest expenses and is the most expensive thing you hope to never use. You absolutely need insurance, but you can also insure yourself to the point of no profit, so exercise good judgement here.

If you own a service business with any employees, workers' compensation insurance will be one of your biggest expenses. Learn about the factors that control it and build training and processes into your business plan to control them. You want your employees to be safe for their own sake. But having systems and training in place to promote safe working conditions and behavior will save you a lot of money and legal headaches.

Lawyers and insurance should be considered the last line of defense in managing risk. The first line of defense is doing the right thing and making sure your employees and managers follow your lead.

Professional services are not the place to drive a hard bargain on price. A fair price for above-average service is a wise investment.

No matter what stage of development your business is in right now, to get to the next one, you have to plan for it. Once you decide to start building your plan, come back to this section often to make sure you are accounting for everything ahead of time.

Oh My!

NuCo
Business Plan

	YEAR 1	YEAR 2	YEAR 3
ORDINARY INCOME / EXPENSE			
Income			
Job Income	200,000	480,000	720,000
Uncategorized Income	0	20,000	30,000
Total Income	200,000	500,000	750,000
Cost of Goods Sold			
Fuel	6,000	15,000	22,500
Vehicle Exp. (oil, repairs, ins.)	2,000	5,000	10,000
Shop Supplies	1,000	2,000	3,000
Labor (tech. pay)	40,000	160,000	240,000
Payroll Tax	32,000	12,800	19,200
Equpment Rental	1,000	4,000	6,000
Truck Payment	9,000	18,000	27,000
Job Supplies	70,000	175,000	270,000
Total COGS	132,200	391,800	597,700
GROSS PROFIT	**$67,800**	**$108,200**	**$152,300**

OVERHEAD

Expense

Background Check	200	1,000	1,500
Drug Testing	100	500	750
Advertising / Social Media	2,000	2,000	4,000
Rent	0	0	18,000
Legal and Accounting	15,000	2,000	3,000
Computer, Internet, Phone, Software	10,000	2,000	5,000
Insurance; Worker's Comp, Liability, Auto	8,000	15,000	23,000
Health Insurance	12,000	12,000	12,000
Office Expenses	500	1,000	5,000

Payroll Expenses

Office Salary	0	0	0
Office Hourly	0	10,000	40,000
Total Overhead	47,800	45,500	109,250

NET INCOME

NET INCOME	**20,000**	**62,700**	**43,050**

Employees

Technicians	1 + ½	4	6
Office	you	you + ¼	you + 1
Trucks	1 ($750/mo)	2	3

Definitions and Key Ideas

- **Accrue:** to make provisions for a charge at the end of a financial period or for work that has been done but not yet paid for.

- **Accrual basis accounting:** an accounting method that measures the financial performance of a company by recognizing sales and expenses when they are billed, rather than when cash transactions occur. (Compare to cash basis accounting.)

- **Amortization:** the reduction in value of certain assets like loans and intangible assets on the books over a period of time.

- **CapEx requirements:** money required to finance the physical assets needed (property, equipment, buildings, etc.) in order for a company to grow their business.

- **Cash basis accounting:** an accounting method where sales and expenses are recorded when they are actually paid for. (Compare to accrual basis accounting.)

- **Cash flow:** the total amount of money (actual cash or equivalent) coming into and out of a business, especially as it affects liquidity.

- **Line of credit (LOC):** an amount of credit extended to a borrower usually secured by accounts receivable (existing sales).

- **Liquidity:** a business's immediately accessible cash, as opposed to assets and other less tangible items of value.

- **Profit & loss statement (P&L):** a standard accounting report that shows a company's revenues and expenses during a given period — usually a month, quarter and year.

- **Pro forma:** an estimate of revenue and expenses for a period of time.

Definitions and Key Ideas (continued)

- **Quality of earnings analysis:** a detailed assessment of all the components of a company's revenue and expenses.

- **Working capital:** money required to operate a business.

- Build a quality team of experienced business professionals; namely a lawyer, accountant, insurance agent and banker.

- Professional services are not the place to drive a hard bargain on price. A fair price for above-average service is a wise investment.

- Have a detailed business plan. It is better to deal with harsh realities in the planning stage than in real life. Any expense you miss will mean less profit for your business.

- Profit on paper is not cash on hand.

- Running out of operating cash is a common cause of failure for small businesses, so build a cash flow statement in addition to the business plan.

4

Nuts and Bolts

Threat of uncertainty that comes right after buying a business
reminds me of bringing our first baby home from the hospital
and realizing there's no owner's manual to go with it. Starting
a business from scratch isn't any easier than caring for a newborn.
No matter how much you plan, things will happen that you are not
expecting. But just like a new baby, your business will let you know
what needs to happen for it to grow. If you don't pay bills on time, folks
will call. Make a mistake on payroll? I promise you will hear about it.
This chapter covers some of the most basic issues you will undoubtedly
run into as a small business owner.

These days, paperwork is a quaint idea. All of the systems and "paperwork" (back office information) I discuss in the following sections are
now often collected remotely on an electronic device by the technician,
sometimes while still on the job. Nevertheless, the following discussion
on data — why it is important and how it is used — is still valuable.

At Desert, we called the paperwork our technicians filled out for a job, a "ticket." Tickets included customer information (name, point of contact, phone number, email, etc.), hours worked, specific tasks completed and the location of the job. Your information may vary, but you will undoubtedly need a system that collects details for each job.

We used log sheets that tracked and listed who the technician was, what hours they worked, what the job was, where it was and the customer's information. Tickets were double-checked against this "master" list, and invoices were created based on that information. Each office kept its own list and made sure all its invoices were submitted each month.

At Desert, a manager always made sure an accurate invoice was generated for each job. This guaranteed we were not paying expenses for work we had not billed.

Labor is usually the largest expense in a service company, so watch that closely. This sounds simple, but the execution can be more difficult than expected. Even with an app or a point of contact system, you still need to make sure the person providing the service fills out the job log in a timely manner so the work is billed out to the customer. Technology should make accountability easier, but you still need to keep a close eye on the whole process to make sure it's working.

Our techs put in long hours and moved heaven and earth to get the job done. But they didn't like doing paperwork and their managers don't tend to enjoy micromanaging employees. Our average daily invoice per job was $2,000. I swear, it would give me heart palpitations to see job tickets floating around the cab of a tech's pickup truck, conjuring visions of wadded-up thousand-dollar bills flying out the window.

Process Check: Revenue vs. Outstanding Invoices

Pay close attention to your revenue. Doctors are notorious for getting into financial binds when their administrative team falls behind, leaving hundreds of insurance claims not submitted and bills unpaid. While the doctor is busy working *in* the business taking care of patients, and the front desk is checking patients in and putting out their own fires, no one is there to make sure the patients are paying. Doctors may not fall into the category of a typical trade-based business, but this common (and very serious) predicament is an indicator of why it's so important to stay on top of billing. At Desert, it seemed like every time we fired a tech, we'd find job tickets in their work truck that had never been submitted. Even though we had a system in place to prevent that,

I learned the hard way there was no perfect solution for making sure we were getting paid for all our work.

Profits are small and all losses are big.

Don't wait until you are cleaning out an ex-employee's work truck, or a year-end audit to discover problems. Require a copy of the profit and loss statement and a balance sheet from your bookkeeper or accountant every month. Familiarize yourself with the details of your business so you can spot anything out of the ordinary. What you see when you check in with your employees on a regular basis should match what you see on your financial reports. If everyone at your company is working and busy but you are not making a profit, start digging for answers. If you have inventory, compare that with the balance sheet. Look out for inanimate objects growing legs and walking off the premises. Obviously, you'll want to keep track of expensive items. But losing a lot of small things can make a big dent in your profit, too. Always ask yourself: Is what I see consistent with our financials?

Process Check: Revenue vs. Expenses

Always know the true cost of your product when setting prices.

A few years ago, a friend of mine who owned a service company came to me for help. He was frustrated that while he had racked up $1 million in sales during the first four months of the year, he was not making any money. I met up with his senior technician and asked him how business was going. He said they were going crazy installing equipment. So, if there was plenty of work being done and equipment being sold, why were they losing money? I checked their books and found the cost data they used for billing out equipment was, at times, 30 to 60 days old. That might fly in some businesses, but in this one, prices increase unexpectedly. One of their most popular services was being billed at $2,700, but the company was paying $3,200 for the labor and supplies to execute it! You can't solve that profit problem with more volume. The fix was simple: Every time an item was purchased, the latest price was entered into the invoicing system and the price for the service adjusted accordingly. The lesson? Review your **profit and loss statements** each month. Does the month's activity match the profit? If not, dig into the details.

Avoid a Financial Wreck

"I never thought he would steal from me." "I trusted him." "He had been with me a long time." Unfortunately, a bookkeeper stealing from the company is a common story. But it's also preventable. I would never defend this type of corrupt behavior, but as a matter of understanding why good folks go bad, consider a bookkeeper's point of view. Working for an owner living large with fancy cars, second homes and expensive clothes, a relatively low-paid employee with their hands on the money could be tempted. Add trusting owners who rely heavily on the back office (and don't check in on a regular basis) and you have a recipe for embezzlement. There are a thousand ways to steal from an unwary owner. I will not even begin to cover them. The good news is that corruption can be mitigated by establishing controls and procedures that prevent it.

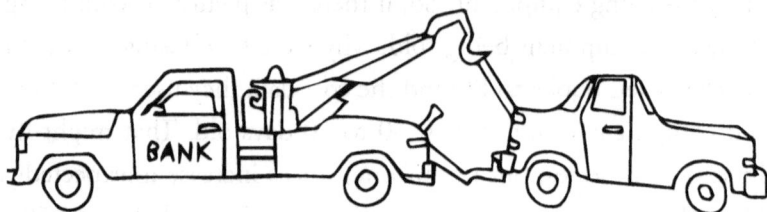

Checks and Bills

A stack of company checks might as well be a pile of cash sitting around. Keep those checks under a lock and key that only you control. Review the accounts payable list every week and provide just enough checks for the bookkeeper to cover those bills. Padding an existing supplier bill is a common way funds can be stolen from a company. You should know what each vendor provides and develop a sense of what a normal price is for their product or service.

Personally sign each check. Money can make people do stupid things. Requiring two signatures for all checks is a common way business partners combat this problem, but even that system has its flaws. Your best defense against losing control of your finances is to pay very close attention to money going out of your account.

Review your bank statement each month to see what checks have been cashed and compare this with your own records of the bills you have paid, paying attention to the vendor and the amount. Investigate any discrepancies immediately. If you are personally not able to maintain this level of scrutiny, find an employee (other than the one in charge of paying the bills) to check for you. It's more likely for one person to go bad than for two parties to team up and steal. Design a system that uses two unrelated people(if they are single, make sure they are not secretly dating) to manage your checks and balances.

Reserves

In addition to your normal "working capital" to cover ongoing operations, create "reserve accounts" that hold cash. A **reserve account** is used in the event of an emergency or an unexpected opportunity. It will also help you operate through slow periods and give you the ability to quickly ramp up supplies and payroll when the opportunity presents itself. How much should you keep in such a reserve? It depends on the size of your business and the length and depth of cycles in your industry. In some cases, we would keep a year's worth of payroll and inventory, which made for a comfortable safety net and a good night's sleep. A very successful friend of mine uses the rule of eight. The number eight is a go-to for many situations in the military when they want to ensure that they have sufficient capacity to carry out a task. For example, if the enemy is bringing one tank and you absolutely have to win the battle, you need to bring eight tanks. For a safe reserve account, start with eight months of cash to meet expenses. At some point, you will have to decide on the appropriate amount for your business based on peak and slow periods.

Marketing

Private equity buyers have told me they consistently find that small companies do not spend enough money or time on marketing. Like most small business owners, I don't think we put enough emphasis on marketing at Desert. However, our branding efforts kept our values in front of employees and customers around the clock. With logos on our trucks working as drivable billboards and on uniforms at job sites, our goal was to get our name and values in front of our customers every chance we had. This approach is somewhat limited to local, trade-based service businesses, so by all means, exploit it to your advantage! TV ads, print, radio and other media methods did not fit our needs as we had a select customer base that would call for our services, but every company is different. Think about who your customer is and how and where you can reach them. Then, budget the time and/or resources it will take to market your services.

Do your service techs working with customers wear a uniform? Don't miss the opportunity to advertise by sending your well-qualified technicians to work with customers wearing your company logo on a shirt or a hat while they're at it. Make sure anyone who has contact with customers has branded business cards with a company logo and information on how to reach them.

Tips for a Good Web Presence

These days, you need a website that will serve as a home base for anyone who thinks to search for your services online. Even if your business model is not internet-focused, having a good website is a relatively inexpensive way to show potential customers what services you have to offer.

Make sure your website is relevant and updated — hire a professional photographer to take pictures that represent the service your business provides. Delegate the responsibility of maintaining the website to someone on your team or hire an outside firm to handle it. If it applies, monitor the status of online customer reviews on sites like Yelp, Google My Business and Facebook Business. Encourage your customers to write reviews and make sure someone on your team has the responsibility of following up on any reviews that indicate superior service was not provided.

Regardless of your industry, social media creates a platform for sharing a positive work experience that will reach more than just an immediate circle of friends and family. Give your employees a reason to tell everyone they know about how great their job is.

Vendor Relationships: Fast Pay Makes Fast Friends

As a business owner, you will always be in the position of waiting to get paid. You pay for inventory, supplies, wages for services and installation. Then, you wait and wait and wait to get paid after you invoice your customers. Net thirty days on the invoice stretches into sixty, then ninety. You start to question if you will ever get paid. Growth in sales makes the effects of slow-paying on cash flow even worse. It won't take you long to really appreciate it when customers pay quickly. Sometimes small businesses try to finance their operation on the backs of their suppliers by slow-paying them. Paying on time will result in your ability to get supplies when there are shortages while your slow-paying competitors will be a lower priority. This situation will happen eventually in any industry, often at a critical time.

Good relationships with suppliers and other vendors are key to growing and differentiating your company from competitors.

There were a few times when our key vendors were in a bind and I was glad to help them out by paying quickly or ordering extra goods we would use later. It really made a difference for them. When the tables turned and we needed supplies or equipment, they would bend over backwards to help us. This gave us the ability to provide service when our competitors could not, a significant factor that contributed to growth at Desert.

Paying on time is paramount to building relationships with your suppliers. But understanding that you are all in this together and cultivating stronger bonds when the opportunity presents itself will take you further. Once, a key vendor located on the Gulf Coast was hit by a hurricane. As soon as I found out, I called, offering to pay all of our outstanding invoices immediately if it would help them get back on their feet. Fortunately, their business had sufficient reserves to weather the storm. Reaching out and letting them know that I was concerned and that we were willing to pay up any outstanding invoices in the wake of disaster did a lot for our relationship.

I can't prepare you for everything that you will need to know, but the information in this chapter is foundational to operating a well-balanced business. There is no shortcut for staying on top of paperwork, regardless of advances in technology. Profits are small and all losses are big. Design processes to watch the details.

- **Profit and loss statement:** a standard accounting report that shows company's revenues and expenses during a given period — usually a month, quarter and year.

- **Reserve account:** money set aside to be used in the event of an emergency or an unexpected opportunity.

- Technology should make accountability with invoices easier, but you still need to keep a close eye on the whole process to make sure it's working.

- Don't scrimp on marketing.

- Build processes for your business that help things run efficiently and profitably.

- Pay particular attention to labor and material costs.

- Check revenue versus outstanding invoices and make sure completed work gets billed and paid.

- Good relationships with suppliers are key to growing and differentiating your company from competitors.

5

Culture

It takes more than a paycheck to retain employees. Creating
an environment where people look forward to work every
day is the root of positive, productive company culture.
Providing an outstanding workplace also helps you attract the
talent necessary to grow. Maintaining a place to work where
everyone is valued should be top priority.

Before Allison and I married, we took a class at the Presbyterian
Church on how to build a healthy marriage using a set of values they called the Four F's: faith, family, finances and frolic. At
Desert, we didn't see the need to encourage frolicking, so I chose a
new set of values guided by the F's to create our company culture.

Faith, family, finances and fellowship were the foundation
of the culture at Desert. These values guided my approach to
management and my interaction with employees, encouraging
goodwill in every aspect of our business.

How do you build a culture using these values? Consider yourself a mirror and expect your employees to reflect your behaviors. As owner, I knew I was taking on tremendous responsibility by hiring people and committing to providing a livelihood for them. I operate on a moral code I learned from basic Christian values. If I wanted the company culture to reflect the F's, I had to lead by example.

Along with faith, family is important to me, and I knew family was important to my employees, too. We did what we could to provide support for employees who needed extra time to tend to family needs outside of the workplace. Once hired, teaching our employees about finances (specifically profit and saving during the good times in the oil patch) was a priority and constant theme at Desert. Food provided an opportunity for fellowship, giving everyone in the company opportunities to connect.

At Desert, I didn't wear my religion on my shirtsleeve or expect anyone else to align with my particular brand of beliefs. I wanted the folks that worked directly for me (and those that worked indirectly with Desert) to feel like they were treated right. My sense of right and wrong came from a Christian upbringing. I appreciate that people from other faiths and backgrounds have a similar sense of right and wrong. When someone on our team or one of their family members was sick or experiencing duress in their lives, I would quietly go to them and let them know I was praying for them. I could see many of my employees' spirits lift through tough times, knowing the boss cared. Prayer is powerful. It wasn't a marketing gimmick: rather, a simple act of faith that helped form the culture I wanted.

Higher Calling

Customers and employees are drawn to organizations that identify a higher sense of purpose. At Desert, we inspected welds for mechanical integrity on oilfield pipelines. Where is the higher calling there? Seems like a pretty dirty, blue-collar job. Yes, it was a job that required hard work in tough conditions, but by doing it well, we prevented pipeline leaks that could lead to environmental and economic disasters for our customers. Our inspection work ensured that friends and family who worked in the industry were safe around high-pressure pipes and explosive hydrocarbons. What could be more important than protecting the people you love? Talking about the higher calling our service provided gave our employees a sense of purpose beyond a paycheck.

Identify the higher calling in your company and build it into your brand. This gives your employees a way to talk about their job with pride while raising the value of the services you provide. It will also make you feel good to go to work every day.

Creating a Work Family

Near the end of the first year after we bought Desert, the owner of one of our biggest competitors called up my operations manager, saying he would put us out of business in six months. Nothing I could have done would have motivated my manager or our technicians more — the guy that called was known in the industry for being a jerk to his employees. Within our first year, we had already established a culture of appreciation, respect and gratitude. We also invested heavily in educating and training our employees. Someone threatening our work family pulled everyone closer together to provide superior service. Business only got better for us after that threat.

I once had a boss who said, "We settle up with our employees every two weeks." That hard-nosed attitude never got folks to do the right thing. It's always worthwhile to take the time and energy to build a work family. In my experience, employees will make decisions that are best for their company because they don't want to let down their work family, friends, coworkers and boss. **Creating a work family and giving people a career over "just a job" leads employees to do what is best for the company, knowing they will also benefit from the company's success.**

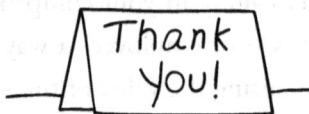

Thank You!

Attitude of Gratitude

Look for opportunities to catch your employees doing something right. Showing gratitude is a big factor in creating an environment where people want to work. A simple "thank you" is a good place to start. Making sure your employees know how much you value their work goes a long way. Some bosses say their employees don't need to be thanked for "just" doing their job, that saying "thank you" should be reserved for someone doing something "above and beyond." Forget that! Make thanking people a **sincere** habit and others will follow suit. Feeling respected and appreciated will hold and keep employees a lot longer than a few bucks extra pay.

Good people can always quit for more money, so you have to make them want to stay.

You have the ability to manage the people around you (and your life) by finding reasons to be thankful. Even if you don't own a business, take an attitude of gratitude with you to your job — take it home, too. It can be life changing. When you make a point of letting those around you know how greatly they are appreciated (while constantly acknowledging what you have to be grateful for), people will pick up on your style and start to do the same. An attitude of gratitude is caught not taught!

Just Tell Me!

When something went wrong, I had a rule for my employees: "Just tell me!" It's always best to bring issues out into the open, especially when it comes to your work family. Build a culture where approaching the management with problems and ideas is the standard. Without this precedent, employees may wait until you sense something is wrong, which will make it more difficult to fix. **Making yourself approachable and open to ideas will set the stage for open communication.**

"Just tell me" only works if you know that you cannot "kill the messenger." If someone brings you bad news, deal with the problem. Do not deal with the person in a negative way. "Hard on problems, soft on people" is a good guideline. Remember, this is a learning opportunity for both of you. Perhaps training or guidance is needed for the employee; maybe you need to change a process on the management side. The point is, it's better to know about these issues than it is to be out of the loop. If you deal with the messenger negatively, it will kill the flow of information.

"Prevent Defense"

Playing "prevent defense" means spotting potential issues before they become big problems and taking steps to keep them from getting out of hand. Problems can be solved much faster if they're caught early on, rather than after they've spread through your organization.

The saying, "One bad apple can spoil the whole barrel," is as true in the workplace as it is in the pantry. With that in mind, there are a few things you can do to prevent naysayers from circulating negative energy. First, make it known upon hiring, and then on a regular basis, that **if anyone has a problem with the company or their assignment they should never complain to a coworker. Encourage your employees to come to you or a manager because, unlike their coworkers, you have the ability to solve it.** Beyond establishing that baseline rule, coaching by walking around is your most basic line of defense. Make yourself approachable so employees can talk to you about issues as they arise. Take action when your employees come to you. That could mean rethinking a rule or guideline or taking the time to explain, from your perspective, why that rule exists. It could also mean facilitating or mediating a conversation with another employee or manager. I found that when a disgruntled employee was given the chance to be heard, or someone explained the reasoning behind a decision or a change, the problem usually went away. Often, major changes are the source of employee concerns, so it's wise to run ideas up the flagpole, asking a broad spectrum of trusted employees to weigh in before implementing them. This allows you to consider perspectives across varying levels of the company and proceed with as little disruption as possible.

One of the best supervisors I ever had taught me that "When two people talk about money, one leaves unhappy." Be upfront with your employees. Make sure they know to discuss pay needs with their manager, not their peers. I have seen companies lose multiple employees over a short period of time because one or two bad apples spread their unhappiness to their peers. This can destroy organizational capability that takes years to build.

One thing I did not like about working at the big company before Desert was that no one would tell the boss (seemingly at any level) when they were wrong. I saw billion-dollar deals done at top levels when the technical staff knew from the start that they would lose money. All the while, every minion on the payroll put a positive spin on the deal to make an executive sound smart. Years later, no one would be held accountable when the project failed to meet expectations. I didn't want that culture. I wanted my employees to "just tell me!"

Growing Careers

Most small companies start with their employees wearing many hats. If you want to grow, you will have to manage the transition from **a team of generalists to a bigger team of specialists**. Invite employees to take part in company growth by investing in their future with training and coaching. Sharing a vision of growing their career builds loyalty. This provides you the opportunity to give your employees a career and not just a job. Investing in people by offering specific training will position them to eventually lead groups or departments as the company grows.

Not My Job!

As you grow, there will always be responsibilities and situations that fall between specific job descriptions, so make sure that everyone is willing to do whatever it takes to help the team. Watch out for the specialists who might be tempted to put their job in a box by specifically adhering to their job description alone, not taking responsibility outside that definition. Like sandlot football, you want everyone to be able to pass, run or block if necessary. You don't want your employees saying, "That's not my job!"

Make Profit Part of Your Culture

One of the most important elements of our company culture was to focus on profit. Invest in educating your team on how their job fits into the financial structure of the company. Folks need to know how their use of time and materials impact the bottom line.

At Desert, we joked that our mission statement was "We are here to make money!" Which was often explained using the following formula, the basis for many discussions concerning profit:

REVENUE – EXPENSES = PROFIT

Get your entire company to think about mistakes and expenses, and how they impact profit. We started by pointing out that most companies do not even make ten percent profit. Knowing that, managers could identify mistakes as costing ten times that in lost revenue. For example, if a crew member lost a $10 lock and key, then the entire hour the crew worked (at $100 per hour) was for nothing as far as the company was concerned. When they had to spend a couple of hours going back to the shop for supplies because they forgot something, the entire day was wasted. At our glass company, breaking a single pane or mirror that cost $300 lost the day's profit for the crew.

Pointing this out repeatedly taught everyone that mistakes and screw-ups actually cost the company ten times the cost of the mistake in revenue. Understanding this caused a shift in behaviors and became a defining characteristic of our culture.

Profits are small and losses are large!

Explain to your employees the impact of saving on profit. If profit is ten percent of revenues, saving just one percent of revenue would increase profits by ten percent. This may not be an easy concept for some, but numbers show how powerful saving on expenses can be to your bottom line.

If the actual profit you make from one dollar of revenue is ten cents, then saving just one penny in expenses on that original dollar will mean a 10 percent addition to your profit.

Initially, many of our employees assumed the owner made all the money between what they got paid and what the company charged for their services. This disconnected them from the reality of expenses. I made an effort to teach our employees how they could minimize error and maximize profit. Sometimes, they could control the time it took to do a task or a job. Profit is made up of pennies on each dollar earned, so managing the little things is key. The time and effort it takes to train each person in the company will pay off when it comes to profitability.

It's your job to educate employees at all levels about making a profit.

Wasting money has always rubbed me the wrong way. I was raised with the concept of "good value." We didn't buy the cheapest things; we shopped around for the best combination of cost, life expectancy and usefulness. Many families do not openly discuss money or finances. I knew it was imperative that I have that discussion with our employees if they were to be expected to handle money the way I did. Being regarded as a tightwad made folks wary of spending money around me. We emphasized spending on good value as opposed to the cheapest alternative, careful not to waste precious cash at every turn.

Safety, Quality, Service

At the end of the day, the values that define your culture will drive how you deliver your product or service to the customer.

Safety, Quality and Service were clear in our branding at Desert. We used those differentiating factors to guide our decision-making process on every level. With a few words, we captured what was most important to our customers and to the success of our company. Safety, Quality and Service were derived from our values, and served as the foundation of our culture, one easily applicable to any service company. In a world where customers are quick to commoditize nearly everything to get companies to compete on price, providing something more is critical. They'll pay a premium if you deliver.

SAFETY — was an outgrowth of the value I placed on **Family**. In this case, that means our work family and our family in the community. I didn't want anyone to get hurt, period. Not just because all businesses want a good safety record to minimize lawsuits and lower insurance costs, but because we cared about our employees' well-being. I often reviewed my interpretation of Safety, Quality and Service with new hires so there was no doubt in anyone's mind how important it was that they return home safe and healthy each night. Stopping folks on their way to a job site to ensure they had the right equipment did more to reinforce safety than any lecture.

QUALITY — can be all encompassing. There is a spectrum of what a quality job looks like. I held high standards, wanting our employees to do just a little better in each aspect of their job. Following the golden rule — treat others as one wants to be treated — we focused on providing our customers with our best work.

When we started in 1999, customers in the oil patch were still inspecting the minimum amount (usually 10 percent) of welds required by law. They often threw their records away at the end of the job, using an invoice to prove they had done the bare minimum. We created an innovative system that recorded inspection data with more detailed results, providing our customers with directions for preventative and corrective actions. We also instituted frequent on-site inspections of our technician's work. These commitments made us a leader in the inspection industry, differentiating our company from our competitors.

The industry changed quickly after we bought Desert, and as I had predicted, the quality of inspection became the most critical element to customers. We had positioned Desert ahead of most of the mom and pop competition by providing our own in-house training.

I saw an opportunity to grow if I could convince our customers to inspect more of their welds. I started a campaign to accomplish that, taking a page from the "quick oil change" business, which has convinced the public to change their oil every 3000 miles even though no owner's manual or manufacturer ever suggested changing oil this frequently. Over time, several of our major customers adopted significantly higher standards because of that. **One of my favorite tactics was to ask a customer how they would feel in front of a Senate investigation or reporter, admitting they had only done the legal minimum to avoid the event of a pipeline spill or plant explosion.** I would point out that they were already paying for having the crew out there, so inspecting a higher percentage of welds was a minor, incremental expense, and a good value. Even if an inspection prevented the most minor leak or smallest explosion, it would save the customer face, not to mention a tremendous amount of money. This was my effort to create demand. In this case, it was also the right thing to do.

SERVICE — was often a hard sell to the technicians and their assistants. It conflicted with an inclination in some to do the very least to earn their pay. When our employees started thinking about their job as a career, they were more likely to embrace the concept that providing good service was also good for them in the long run. Good service required extra effort not seen by management, so it was difficult to measure directly. Our approach was simple: If a customer asked for the same crew back, then they must have provided great service. I spent a lot of time in my pitch to new hires and during safety meetings explaining how both the employees and the company benefitted each time we were called back by a customer for another job.

In a business as cyclical as inspection, the techs and their assistants would realize quickly that providing good service rewarded everyone involved. When technicians embraced the concept of providing superb service, we really began to grow, acquiring repeat customers and more work by word of mouth. We were able to improve our profits dramatically by not having to compete with other inspection companies. Sharing those profits by giving modest rewards to crews when the customer requested them specifically reinforced the work ethic and ethos we were after. We were always looking for good value and we wanted the same for our customers.

Managing from a Perspective of Abundance

A mainstay of our culture at Desert, and a factor that gave us quite an advantage, was a concept I call managing from a perspective of abundance. A company with a culture of abundance does not fight with its employees over "the pie" as if the pie is a fixed size. Instead, I instilled a different attitude: "We are all in this together."

My daughter worked at a company that gave $5 Christmas bonuses to their employees while the bosses took home tens of thousands of dollars in bonuses and went on business retreats to fancy resorts. I was not surprised or disappointed when she quit for a better opportunity.

Executives that believe in a world of scarcity are often mired in the "I win, you lose" mentality. This leads to suspicion and fighting that drains the energy from everything. When folks at the top treat themselves excessively well at the company's expense while those working on the front lines get scraps, poor customer service and a high turnover are inevitable.

In a world of abundance, you believe that by working together, both sides can grow, resulting in more for both the owner and the employee. Many times, in order to provide better service for the customer, an employee must work overtime. This improves the quality of service while allowing the company to charge a premium rate. That means the employee makes more money, too. This is in sharp contrast to a company that does not allot for overtime, which often results in poor customer service. Companies that fight over revenue and pay are often slow to grow. Businesses committed to a perspective of abundance make for a nicer environment and are often more successful.

To put the concept of abundance into action I created a system of *rewards and recognition.* To a hard-working employee, recognition is just as important as money. Don't miss an opportunity to highlight their efforts. Sometimes that recognition involves money, but it may also involve opportunities for career growth. Maintain the idea that a financially strong company with a good reputation benefits everyone.

Business Blessings from Abundance

Early on at Desert, we had a lot of debt and I would dread making that bank payment each month. I would operate at levels *beyond* frugal. We would laugh about certain companies being lean and mean; we were skinny and vicious.

A single pickup truck was a huge expense for us. My operations manager, having always worked in a company where money was tight, would not recommend buying one until he was certain he could keep it working 100 percent of the time. I viewed things differently. For example, if I put more money into the company by buying more trucks, I would eventually get more out of the investment. So, I started keeping a spare truck around. My operations manager hated seeing it just sitting there, so it was constant motivation for him to keep it out on a job.

Of course, the cost was much more than just the capital cost of the truck, because we had to keep a crew employed to man the truck and do the work. Keeping extra people around when money was tight was a hard sell for me, but it ended up being one of the greatest catalysts for growth. Too often, small companies don't have time for training, safety, time off, etc. By having extra hands, we were able to develop skilled technicians at a faster rate, a key factor in the growth of our business.

Extra hands gave us the opportunity to provide training to relatively new employees, making them feel like a valued part of our work family. It also meant that we were able to give our technicians time off to take care of personal business. Service companies in the oil patch have a tendency to run their techs nonstop when it's busy. Our move to make time for training and personal needs set us apart from competitors, making us the preferred employer. The most important factor was that it allowed us to provide superior service. Our customers could count on us to have the people and equipment available to handle any rush job. **Our ability to handle those emergency jobs brought us goodwill** and put Desert on their speed dial.

Recognition and Reward

I took the best of what I learned from Amoco's recognition and rewards program and built a system proven to generate superior work from employees anywhere I've tried it. Managing and motivating your team to get the outcome you want is one of the most important jobs you will have as a business owner. Do this well and results, profit and growth will follow.

Early on, a friend suggested that every owner should walk around with $100 bills in their pocket to give employees when he or she saw them doing something good. I took his advice, making sure to focus on rewarding behaviors I wanted to see repeated. Cash aside, the recognition — which was much more important in the long run — motivated employees more than the reward. With this approach, make sure your managers know that recognition is done in public while criticism should always be kept private.

Any time I gave a reward or public recognition, I made it clear it was not a gift; I emphasized how the individual had earned that R&R. Gifts in the workplace can come across as condescending or arbitrary when they are given without clarification. Making it about productivity and performance, even if it's just someone doing their job, is key.

Sometimes, I refer to money as "grease." As a student, I learned that **a few dollars at just the right time was much more valuable than a lot of money when you really didn't need it**. Like grease, a little applied in the right spot can make things run a lot smoother. Helping your employees with unexpected costs, when a few bucks can make a difference for them, builds loyalty and a sense of family. I purposely didn't attach any expectations to my giving; it was total free will. If you are coaching by walking around, you'll know when your employees are working hard. You'll be in tune to when they have an upcoming trip, birthday, wedding, personal emergency or new baby on the way. A little extra at the right time is really appreciated.

Giving someone $100 as extra spending money on vacation or to take a loved one out to dinner goes a long way. Look for opportunities to reward your employees so they get to explain to friends and family the reason behind it. Think about it: You give your employee $100 and she takes someone out for dinner with it. They talk about why she was given $100, which reinforces her good work and shows your company is a good place to be employed. Put a line item in your budget for recognition and reward. This makes sure you and your managers put this concept into practice.

Once, after a great month of business, I bought a case of expensive champagne and walked around the office giving each person a bottle. I heard about those bottles being used for special occasions and celebrations for a long time. I hope when those bottles were opened, my employees recounted the story of how great it was to work at Desert.

Did this extra effort to recognize employees make a difference? Absolutely! Several times, I would have a tech get mad and
quit over something minor. This is a common occurrence in the
blue-collar world, because techs can always find another job. This
aspect of the workforce was eye-opening to me, since I had only
worked in a big company office before Desert. Fortunately, my
habit of extending extra consideration to my employees (and their
families), had an interesting effect. Often, they would come back
the next day and ask for their job back. Seems it was common for
their spouse or partner to remind them how well I had treated
them and their family compared to other employers.

These relatively minor ways of recognizing your hard-working
team can be some of the most satisfying parts about owning a
business. Sometimes, $100 wasn't sufficient to reward an employee
for outstanding service. We dealt with larger scale accomplish-
ments accordingly.

When a crew's outstanding work resulted in a special request to
work on the same construction company's next project, I always
reminded them that what was good for the crew was good for the
company. Occasionally, a crew would hit a home run, maybe, for
example, they would be requested as lead truck on a large job.
Some of those contracts were hundreds of thousands of dollars!
I figured that if we had a formal sales force, I would have been
giving a salesman a bonus, so it made sense to give the crew a
bonus instead. That bonus was in line with the price tag of the
new work, often several thousand dollars. Naturally, it inspired
practices beneficial for the crews and the company, encouraging a
culture rooted in superior service.

At the glass company, it's not unusual for Corey to show up on
the job site to hand out $100 bills. He has great field hands that

have bailed him out of many tough situations where they were running behind the construction schedule and had to make up time. By passing out cash, he recognizes his employees for stepping it up for the whole team. After all, the company's reputation for outstanding service is being built in the field. Sometimes, when work takes folks out of town on birthdays or anniversaries, he sends their spouse up to join them, making it extra special by upgrading the hotel and covering a nice meal.

Our method of special consideration at Desert set us apart from large companies who were seen as impersonal — forced into treating everyone the same to keep human resources (and the lawyers) happy. At Amoco, any time someone was treated differently, for better or worse, HR and the lawyers worried about discrimination lawsuits. In a small company, you can treat folks differently because their strong performance is easy to identify (and defend if necessary). This is one of the many perks of working for a small company.

Boss Cook

It's common for companies to take employees out for lunch to celebrate. I think it's a good practice. To make celebrations around company performance more meaningful, I kicked it up a notch by cooking for the whole shop. This included doing the shopping, set-up and cleanup. My shrimp boils were a hit! I got the sense that our team liked seeing the boss go the extra mile to serve them.

I didn't always do the cooking. On Thanksgiving, we would have a potluck celebration — I fried the turkey and everyone signed up to bring sides and dessert. For Christmas, I brought the ham. Potlucks gave everyone the opportunity to participate and show off their specialties or family recipes. Employees got to know one another beyond small talk in the office or sandwiches out in the field. Eating together fosters solid working relationships among employees. Familiarity allows us to be more comfortable about asking for help or advice with a job task. It also makes space for employees to work out unresolved issues that have been stewing, without involving the boss. Aim for this culture. A team that is comfortable approaching one another with questions and concerns will provide better service and be happier all around.

Find something you do well that you'd like to share with the people working for you. For me, it was putting on a festive shrimp boil. Appreciate and treat your staff well. They'll likely step it up when dealing with coworkers and customers. They will instinctively provide service at the highest level, the same way their boss has served them.

Building Goodwill —
The Payoff for Treating People Right

For a service company, goodwill often accounts for the lion's share of the cost paid for a company. Making an effort to build goodwill should be a focus of your efforts daily. The accounting definition for goodwill is "the difference in the total price of the business and the value of the hard assets." It's called "blue sky" because bankers joke that is what you're paying for — goodwill isn't physical. It is all about the ability to retain your customers, especially the largest ones. It determines whether they will stay with the company even with new owners, or if the key employees that run the business's day-to-day operations stay with the company? That's why you should focus on building goodwill every day.

Goodwill can be enhanced by anyone in the company, not just the owner. That means your relationship with important vendors and suppliers is vital. Keeping both customers and employees is the payoff from running the business with all Four "F's" and a sense of abundance.

Badwill — Making Lemonade

Sometimes there are dark clouds in your blue sky. Having bought several small companies, I have come up with a concept called "badwill." It is just as real as goodwill, but someone selling their company won't mention it. Just like you pay for goodwill when you purchase a company, you also get some measure of badwill. However, if you play your cards right, inherited badwill can make way for real opportunity.

Once, I was trying to get an account with a big gas processing plant. I had driven two hours to see the plant manager who said he was busy when I arrived, so I told him I would wait. After hanging around the small town long enough to eat two meals at Dairy Queen, the plant manager called and asked if I still wanted to meet in a couple of hours or reschedule. He was clearly trying to wait me out, hoping I would give up and go home. Finally, well after normal business hours, I got to see him. I think he was impressed that I had invested so much time just to shake hands. He listened to me talk about buying the company and wanting to work with him. Then, he asked if the previous owner had anything to do with my new company. I assured him the old owner was out of the picture, at which point he proceeded to divulge every problem he ever had with our company. He had vowed never to work with Desert again.

After listening to him vent for quite some time, I told him I couldn't do anything about the past, but that we would try and conduct business the way he wanted if he gave us another chance. I told him if anything was not up to par with our agreement, he should call me directly and I'd take care of it. We ended up working together for many years.

Your company will make mistakes — how you handle it when things go wrong will differentiate you from your competitors.

We worked hard to build relationships with our customers. At one point, one of my managers was lured away by a competitor unable to build business with his own organization. This former manager and his new boss then approached one of our biggest customers, offering to handle all of their business for 20 percent less. The customer said they were very pleased with the quality of our work, liked our service, and were quite confident we would take care of them as they grew. They were not interested in changing, even for a big price break. In the end, the competitor fired our old manager, who was unable to deliver the business he promised. Needless to say, the competitor had a hard time hiring any more of our people after firing that manager. I hired the manager back. He was my strongest advocate in educating our employees about the perils of quitting to work for the competition. Now *that* is goodwill!

Energy

Keep work fun, positive and uplifting. Being the boss gives you license to do the unexpected, which means you should always be looking for ways to energize your team. I used to start Monday mornings with donuts for everyone, taking 15-30 minutes to catch up and plan for the week. We all preferred that to a formal Monday staff meeting that would drag on too long. The staff often joked that my secret to squeezing more work out of them was loading them up with caffeine and sugar. We kept a large candy jar by the door, and it was seldom empty.

If you can't bring the energy yourself, find those who can and empower them to spread it across the company. Provide them with the resources they need to bring it! Find every reason to celebrate: closing out the end of a month, getting a big stack of work done, someone mastering a new skill, record-high revenues, or no accidents! Occasionally, I would hand out PayDay candy bars and tell everyone we were having two paydays that period. Scratch-off lottery tickets were a fun energizer at Desert, too. Every once in a while, I would ask a brand-new employee if they knew they were eligible for a big bonus. Then, I would say all it took was hard work and a lot of luck before handing them a lotto ticket. It was always funny to me, but everyone's a critic.

Celebrating regularly will give your team even more reason to do a good job for you and the company by making them feel important. In a repressive environment where credit is seldom acknowledged, things seem to go wrong more often. Disgruntled employees consciously and subconsciously find reasons to "get back" at the company. Equipment breaks, things don't get done on time, data gets lost — you get the picture.

Culture is the one thing that cannot be delegated. Managing from a perspective of abundance means growing a bigger pie instead of fighting over each piece. Your employees are assets, not liabilities, so treat them that way. A paycheck is just one way of making sure your team is well taken care of. Recognize and reward good work and behaviors consistent with company values. You'll create a culture that generates more of the same. Make space for fellowship and strong working relationships, allowing room for laughter and good food. It's up to you to find out what is important to your customer, how to differentiate your company and charge a premium price for your services. Lead by example, making sure your managers follow suit. A strong workplace culture will maximize profit and growth.

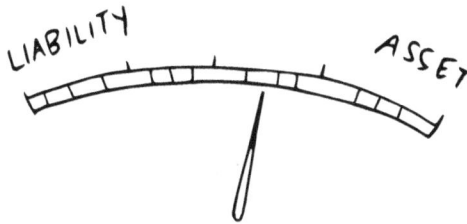

EMPLOYEES

Definitions and Key Ideas

• **Attitude of gratitude:** constantly looking for ways to show that you are thankful to the people around you. An attitude of gratitude is caught not taught!

• **Goodwill:** the ability to retain your customers, especially the largest ones. Will they stay with the company even with new owners?

• Build your company and culture on a set of values that you believe in. In my case it was the Four F's: faith, family, finance, fellowship.

• Identify the higher calling in the service you provide and use it to build your brand.

• It's your job to educate employees at all levels about making a profit.

• Play "prevent defense." Spot potential issues before they become a problem. Make yourself approachable so your employees can come to you with these issues!

Definitions and Key Ideas (continued)

- Good people can always quit for more money, so you have to give them a reason to stay.

- Create a system to recognize and reward your employees for their hard work.

- Helping your employees grow will help your company grow.

- Teach your employees $1 screw-up takes $10 revenue to fix.

- Profits are small, losses are large. Profit is made up of pennies on each dollar earned, so managing the little things is key.

- Safety - Quality - Service: compete on value not price. Demonstrate how you add value to your customer to get better profits.

- Your company will make mistakes. How you handle it when things go wrong will differentiate you from your competitors.

6

On Being the Boss

Everyone dreams of being the boss. When you're at the top, there is no one to tell you how to do things or boss you around. It's all up to you, which can be both exciting and scary as hell. Making decisions that have a major impact on employees can weigh heavily on you. As a boss, you will have to decide whether or not to hire or fire someone, how to adhere to policies and when to give raises and promotions (or not). You will have to learn to manage your feelings when making tough calls. For every personnel decision, you need to be ready to manage the downside. Make your best choice, accept that decision, and fight the urge to second-guess yourself. Go with your gut.

Being the boss certainly puts you under a microscope. Walk the talk! If you deviate from your values, even a little bit, it will undermine your efforts to build a company culture based on those values.

You never really get to "do whatever you want" as the boss. You always have to answer to your customers, and you are bound to standard best practice for business, laws, regulations and the moral struggle of hiring and firing people. Managing change, hiring, training, firing and financing for a small business can be terrifying. This chapter covers my approach to tackling some of these tougher decisions.

Put your capital into the business instead of spending it. Employees always notice. Showing off your new car or boat is not going to motivate the people working for you. This is especially true if they have to make do with old equipment, driving beat-up company trucks, only to watch their fearless leader speed away in a brand-new convertible. If your company is in good shape and you want to spend money, that is fine; just avoid waving it in the faces of your hard-working service techs and field hands. I gained respect from our new employees by driving a modest Toyota while we bought new company trucks for technicians in the field. We budgeted for employee training and development. We also made sure to fund recognition and rewards for the employees, even when times were tough. Folks were always amazed at how easy it was to grow the companies we bought by putting money into training, tools and equipment. I wonder if the previous owner had ever understood the true cost of that boat he bought.

Change: Evolution, Not Revolution

Growth creates change. People don't like it when change puts their paycheck at risk. But you have to evolve to stay in business. Managing change will be one of your biggest challenges, especially when you build organizational capability. The best way to manage change is by sharing your vision and asking any affected employees for input. An organizational assessment tool is not a secret document — sharing it with staff helps map out their career goals as the company grows. When you discuss plans for change, be sure to include the tools, training and other necessary resources your employees will need to adapt and excel. Your employees will want to hear about change from you personally — if you don't deliver the news yourself, the rumor mill will, and people often assume the worst.

And if you don't include the entire team from the get-go, you run the risk of staff sabotaging the "new way," making sure it fails. This was particularly important when working with service techs or field hands. There were many great ideas thought up in the office that didn't translate well to the field. Ideas discussed with service techs prior to implementation had a higher rate of success. Folks working in the field knew to incorporate steps to make a new process physically practical. Other times, when the field hands were not included, ideas failed, because they required unrealistic work demands. By not involving field hands from the beginning, they had less motivation to make an idea work, because it was not theirs.

If you want a new policy, process or practice to work, be sure to include all affected employees in its development.

Growing Panes

When we were thinking about buying the automated frame fabrication machine for the glass company, our project manager did not think it was a good idea. It cost a lot of money, and he really didn't think it would be an improvement over the way we were already doing things. Since he had a lot more experience in the business than either Corey or I, his dissent was cause for caution. We valued his opinion, so we sat down with him and discussed every issue he had. Ultimately, we made the decision to go ahead and buy it. Once it was up and running, it proved to be as great as we hoped, and he became a real fan of the new technology. The outcome might have been different if we chose to make that purchase without hearing him out first. If you don't have the support of the people who will be operating your machinery, even the best equipment can fail.

Finding Good People

One of the best ways to fill critical positions is to "grow your own." Our company needs often grew faster than we could hire, resulting in employees working well beyond their comfort zone during periods of heavy growth. Many of those who stuck it out in this atmosphere earned promotions.

I often ask folks "What keeps your business from growing?" The most common answer is, "I can't find good people." Networking consistently yielded employees who fit into our company culture.

From the tech level to the highest administrative positions, we always considered internal references first. With these hires, much of the vetting had been done before they applied, because techs' friends and family were already familiar with our values. The "sponsor," or employee who referred them, had an automatic, vested interest in their success.

Hiring Diamonds in the Rough

At Desert, we proudly operated with a small staff, considering our company's fast growth. We ran lean to avoid layoffs during slow periods. Growth provided opportunities that resulted in many employees learning on the job. We gave people with modest educational backgrounds the opportunity to shoot for jobs most big companies keep out of their reach. I was comfortable with this because, under pressure, they demonstrated their ability and strong character. We did inherit some good people when we bought Desert. They blossomed with training, honing in on the nuts and bolts discussed in Chapter 4, notably profit and loss.

If you ask them, most job applicants are smart enough to figure out what you want to hear. A standard job interview does little to reveal someone's true nature. I learned more about someone's value system by asking general questions in a comfortable setting and showing empathy for their answers. In my experience, they often expanded upon their answers in a way that provided valuable insight. I wanted to know about my employees' pasts, of specific successes they had in any area. Was their success the result of characteristics we were looking for — tenacity, intelligence, hard work, creativity, etc.? Were they team players or lone wolves? Both have their place. Did they tend to blame others or take responsibility for their mistakes? Were they quick to share success with others involved?

When I interviewed, I would look for STARs, which stands for: Situation, Task, Action and Result. It was a good sign if they talked about a situation where they played an active role and it turned out well. I believe that past performance and personal experience are good indicators of future potential. Look for characteristics and skills, not just experience in one specific task.

I sought people who wanted careers, not just a job — someone who was anxious to make a good life for themselves and their family. I took chances on folks when I saw good character, regardless of an unpolished exterior.

On Coaching

When you have issues with an employee's performance, start by talking with them about it. Can they play another role within your organization? Can you modify their job to fit an alternative schedule or style? One of the benefits of running a small company is that you are not constrained to a particular organizational structure. Sometimes all the employee needs is a change in how things are done. I saw plenty of examples of folks that were fantastic at putting out fires, but anything that took more than a day was a disaster.

A change in assignment sometimes solved this, instead of firing and finding someone new. If they have the core values and fit well in your company culture, it is worth considerable effort to find the right fit for everyone. If the fit is just not there, it is really in the best interest of the employee and the employer to move on, even if it means letting someone go.

Firing

Firing is never easy. Of course, there were cases where the employee was obviously not the right fit for our team. I didn't lose much sleep over firing someone because they couldn't or wouldn't do their job, but I admit I was guilty of keeping folks on while they worked out some personal problems. I would give them the benefit of the doubt that their performance would improve once their personal issues were resolved.

At some point, you will have to fire a good person, maybe even a friend or relative, because it is just not working. This will be one of the toughest things you ever have to do. It comes with the territory of being the boss. Like the phrase goes: "The buck stops here." It certainly does when it comes to the dirty work of firing.

I will never forget the first guy I fired. He came in late every day and took too long to get things done. He was smart and capable, but just not into our line of work. He worked tirelessly at the community theater, building sets and practicing his lines, but did not hold the same enthusiasm for his actual job. I was working late one evening, a few days after his dismissal, when he walked into my office. He had anger in his eyes and I really thought he was going to beat me up! I told him to sit down and tell me off, whatever he had to say, I would listen. After the onslaught, I pointed out that I never thought that he was incapable, but it was clear to me that his heart was not in the work. I asked him if he wasn't happier working on plays than being an engineer. He agreed, realizing this was a chance for him to do what he loved, that he had been trapped by the big paycheck.

He ended up thanking me for my time and, a few weeks later, left town to go back up north where he was from and work in the summer theater. He sent me Christmas cards for years, thanking me for helping him move on to his dream career. I learned that sometimes, letting folks go can help them find a happier path.

Most of the time the results will not be this warm and fuzzy. Be careful of the savior complex. Sometimes, people just can't do the work. If you find yourself even thinking about firing someone, I suggest you go ahead and do it. You have probably waited too long already.

How? Short and quick. It is not a debate; the decision has been made. Have a witness/observer for your discussion so they can take notes. Make sure your witness knows their role is to observe and document, not participate in the discussion. There is no need to make your future ex-employee feel like you are ganging up on them. Tell the employee your decision, and explain why they are being fired. Thank them for working there. Tell them HR will follow up with a discussion of the termination paperwork and process.

At some point, you will have to fire someone. It may be very unpleasant for you and devastating to them *and* their family, but you have to do it. The only reason you are firing someone is because they can't do the work or they don't align with the company values and culture. They have to leave because their attitude and work ethic will spread to other employees, potentially destroying what you have worked so hard to build.

Managing Stress

Firing folks can be gut-wrenching and scary. Hiring, finance, managing change, making payroll, lawsuits and other boss jobs are all stressful. No matter how bad things get, you must be seen as in control of the situation. Your calm demeanor as a leader will give your team the confidence to deal with even the most difficult situations.

Take care of yourself — your employees depend on you. Make ongoing efforts to maintain or improve your physical and mental health. Prepare as if you are getting ready for a big competition; you are.

Start/continue exercising. Do it today; do it every day. Try to get outside. Studies have shown that people who have a physical connection with nature are more resilient. If nothing else, walk around the block every day.

Stress can make people eat crummy stuff, which makes you feel worse. Stay hydrated, and try to eat things that make you feel good in the long run. Watch the alcohol: There are no solutions at the bottom of that bottle. That walk around the block? Take one when you start to feel anxious or stressed. Think about something positive as you go.

Men wait until there is a problem before going to the doctor, but are religious about changing the oil in their car — go figure. Stereotypes aside, if you are responsible for running a company and employing other people, you also need to be responsible for your health. Regardless of your gender, get a thorough annual checkup!

At the end of the day, make a list of the things that went right or that you are grateful for. When things are really tough, make a list of all the good things that have happened in the last year. Make another list of all the good things that have happened in your life. Keep this list along with photos of your family or friends in a place you will look every day as a constant reminder that you are loved.

Sometimes sleep is a problem. Keep a pen and paper next to your bed. When you can't sleep, writing down what ails you can help bring out the solution and keep swirling thoughts at bay.

Being the boss can be lonesome. There are many things you cannot discuss with anyone else. My wife listened to me often, not knowing the details of what I was complaining about, but understanding it would help. My Labrador listened to a lot of my work problems; everything I told her was kept in confidence. Prayer has helped me through many tough times.

Owning a business can be one of the most rewarding things you do in life. You finally get to do things your way! Hiring and firing comes with the territory. Training leaders to uphold your values and act on your behalf is one of the most satisfying components of being boss. After all, you are replicating your values and what you do best. No other endeavor has the potential to grow your company and your success as much as managing your managers well.

this too shall pass

Definitions and Key Ideas

- Put your capital into the business instead of spending it.

- If you want to implement a new policy, process or practice to work, be sure to include all affected employees in its development.

- Go with your gut.

- Managing change will be one of your biggest challenges, especially when you build organizational capability.

- Grow your own! It's the best way to build your workforce.

- Manage Stress: take care of yourself and stay calm. Others depend on you!

7

Managing

The Manager's Perspective

Nearly everything that is good for the company makes a manager's job tougher. In smaller companies, a manager's responsibilities tend to cover managing both employees and customers. Keeping sales up will be one of their most important roles. It's easy for a manager to get more business by reducing service costs for a customer, but that move is bad for the company. Managers are the ones who hear customers complain about price the most. How often do they hear the owner talk about profit? **This chapter covers how to create leaders who reflect the culture and values you have established in your company.**

There will always be a few things in your process that require the boss's expertise. Being away from the office is one way to discover those things. I distinctly remember the anxiety and excitement I felt as I scheduled my first month-long vacation. We rented a house at the beach so I made sure there was a good internet connection and that we were close to an airport in case of emergency. The managers reacted perfectly — instead of feeling abandoned or leaderless, they understood that I trusted them to handle things in my absence. It would have taken quite a calamity for someone to pick up the phone and call me for help. Reaching the stage where you are no longer a critical a part of daily operations is a big milestone and a huge payoff in personal freedom.

Managing Managers

You may find a variance in style between the owner and manager, and likely among managers themselves, but there should be no compromise when it comes to values and company culture. Establish goals and objectives for your leaders that are tied to a bonus program that rewards them for meeting those objectives.

Every business should have what's called a **delegation of authority** form. This is a legal document that spells out the monetary and legal authority given to each manager. Formalizing this information protects both the employee and the business. The company should also have a written emergency plan. If the boss can't show up, who takes on their duties? What are those duties? This document should include an action plan for natural and manmade disasters. The plan should also include what to do if someone gets hurt or a government regulatory agency shows up on location.

The Concept of Value

When managers run into customers complaining about price, it might help to point out that the customer is paid by their company to complain about price; it's their job. Make sure your managers know it's *their* job to push back. Teach them to talk about past jobs, emphasizing superior service and glowing customer reviews as concrete examples during discussions on price. Educate your managers on the full cost of the products and services you provide. Remind everyone in the company, especially managers, that you want to compete on service and quality, **not on price.** Make sure they know that when a business competes on price, wages are lower and benefits are fewer. Good prices and profits are good for the company and for your employees.

When dealing with individuals as customers, things get a bit more difficult. From time to time, you may have to negotiate on price. Focus on value. For many smaller services, if a customer doesn't find a good value, they'll usually just go find another service provider. While you can't track customer data like a big company, you can train yourself and your staff to be very watchful of your customers. Learn to notice any little thing that seems out of the ordinary; a small tip, a disappointed look, a hesitation to pay. If you see anything at all, start a dialogue. What you find out from one customer may reveal what a lot more are thinking. Reward the customer for their help with something, even if it is just a heartfelt thankyou and a promise to do better. A general "Was everything alright?" will generate, "Yup, fine" 99 percent of the time. Instead you should ask: "What was the one thing we could have done better?" You might be surprised at what you hear and you might get real material to improve your service. The key is to ask a specific question relevant to your service or product.

Pay Discussions

One of the hardest parts of a manager's job is telling employees they work with every day that they cannot have a raise. Managers have this conversation with employees all the time. The easiest way to protect your manager from this conundrum is by putting a company policy in place stating that raises are only considered at certain times of the year. Tax season and the start of school seem to be times when employees commonly seek raises. **When it comes to pay, it takes discipline to say no and considerable judgment to say yes.** It's your job to think about process and organization, so you need to give the immediate supervisor an "out" when handling raises by having a line of defense above them (you or HR). This structure preserves the working relationship between employees and their immediate supervisor. However, you should always be on the lookout for exceptions.

Remaining untethered to strict company policies is one of the greatest benefits of owning a business. Small companies can be more responsive to employee emergencies. If an employee says something about needing a raise, it's important that your manager understand the real reason for the request: Do they deserve a higher rate because of added responsibilities? Issues with personal finances? Is your competitor down the road offering more pay for a similar job? Coaching managers to consider these discussions from more than one perspective makes them better leaders.

At service companies, people are your most valuable asset. Therefore, you and your managers should make time to take care of them. A manager's job is much easier if they are not constantly hiring and training replacements.

Finance 101 for Managers

When it comes to managers, "growing your own" will allow individuals to become the kind of leaders your business needs. At Desert, we promoted our operating managers from the field ranks, which required us to teach them how we operated financially.

Train your managers to discuss finances with their team. If you don't, you may wind up with employees who believe that once their salaries are covered, everything else is pure profit. Point out that most companies do not make 10% profit on revenues. Hold regular discussions on major cost components and their relative impact on the company. This gives managers and employees information on the biggest expenses and focuses their work on ways to reduce costs.

At Desert, we segmented financials by office. I could compare major expense categories between offices, and managers could share ideas on how to hold down costs. This system was part of our bonus program and drove multiple offices toward best practices.

REVENUE   PROFIT

A penny saved is a dime earned!

Occasionally, at our manager meetings, I would give each manager $100 in $5 bills. As I explained each major company expense, they would have to pay for it by handing back the equivalent percent of their cash. At the end, they were left with ten dollars (10 percent profit). This exercise also drove home the point that $1 of expenses saved increased profit by $1, a 10 percent increase in profit. Many of the managers kept a $10 bill on their desk — a few even framed it — as a reminder to keep expenses at bay.

How Do You Keep Employees?

Employee retention isn't all about money. In fact, money is low on the list of real reasons people leave. Give this outline to your managers as a guide for how to keep good employees:

1. Show respect by listening to what your employees are saying.

The first step in showing respect is giving your time and attention. Ask for your employees' opinions in matters that concern them or areas where they have expertise. Listen to them. Be quick to recognize when someone makes a contribution, does something particularly well or helps someone else (all good reasons to hand them a $100 bill). When someone approaches you, stop what you are doing and look at them. Ask them clarifying questions. Engage with them.

> *A key employee once told me that he chose to stay with our company — even though a competitor was willing to pay him more — because whenever he came into my office, I closed my laptop, ignored the phone and paid attention to what he had to say. At his interview with our competitor, the manager was constantly multitasking. That annoyed our employee and made him realize he wouldn't have the attention or respect there that he had at our company.*

2. Build a personal relationship with your employees and their families.

Know the names of their spouses, partners, girlfriends, boyfriends and kids. Familiarize yourself with their situation at home so you can give them extra consideration (day-to-day flexibility, time off, etc.) when they need some. Never pass up an opportunity to brag about your employee in front of their family, especially their parents. If your employee is out of town on a job for a long period, you could send a restaurant gift certificate or a nice note to the spouse or partner keeping everything running at home. Flexible work schedules are highly valued by employees — one of the perks a small company can offer to differentiate themselves from big companies. At this juncture, a recognition and rewards program will present opportunities to give employees a little money or extra time off. This foundation of trust and respect goes beyond just knowing about your employees.

If you are quick to do these things for long-term employees and their families, it will likely give new hires incentive to stick around.

3. Emphasize an ongoing relationship with the company.

Keep track of how long your employees have been working with you. Celebrate milestones and tie those back to landmarks associated with company growth. Let each employee know why you couldn't have gotten to where you are now without them. On occasion, discuss your shared values and how you have been through good and bad times. Our competitors at Desert didn't have a process to promote employees to any position beyond the one they were hired for. I would often point out to our employees that of course they were attractive to our competition, because other companies didn't have training and certification programs like ours. This conversation can lead to discussions on career planning.

4. Encourage your employees to visualize their career within your company.

Make sure you and your employees see working at the company as a career and not just a job. Too many trade-based service businesses see their employees as expendable. Treating your employees differently will set you apart from the competition and make you a preferred employer in your industry — a significant competitive advantage. You will be able to hire the best and it will show in your services.

Talk about your employees' goals, the kind of work they enjoy and how the future needs of the company might create opportunities that suit them. Since managers have access to information on growth plans and strategy, they can steer employees toward positions with a forward-thinking, career-based vision. Agreeing on where team members see themselves in the future of the company gives you a common goal to reach.

> *I hired Juliet to be a receptionist at Desert. In her interview, she said she wanted to be an HR professional one day. On her first day, the long-time office manager/bookkeeper left at lunch, never to return. Juliet was instantly promoted to office manager and did a great job. She eventually became an HR manager for the billion-dollar public company that bought us — far beyond the career goal she identified when we first interviewed.*

Often, employees came up with positions that fit better than anything I had thought of on my own. One of our senior technicians who didn't like leaving town and was not up to long hours out in the field suggested he become an internal quality control coach. That position helped us leverage his considerable experience and meet his needs. It also differentiated us from competition, as no other company had a person dedicated to quality control.

Patty Beach, a long-time friend and leadership coach, always says the number one job of a manager is to truly *see* the talents and gifts in their employees. Who they are is the key to who they are becoming. Make sure your managers know it!

5. Play "prevent defense" by being visible and accessible to your employees.

When you make yourself available to your employees, you are more likely to identify problems and find the root of them through daily conversations. Employees should know to come to you with their issues *before* they start talking to their co-workers. Reward them for coming to you first by doing what you can to solve the problem. This could mean re-thinking guidelines or facilitating a discussion with another employee after a disagreement. More often than not, the act of taking the time to respectfully listen to the employee can diffuse a situation. Whatever the case may be, employees must know that the first course of action when they are unhappy about something at work is to talk to you about it.

Look out for people quitting. It is important to pick up on rumors about someone being unhappy with their job. The best practice is to be direct. Call them into your office and ask them if they are thinking of quitting and how far along they are in the thought process. If they are a marginally performing employee, advise them that it's their last day. Too often, when I let them stay, they damaged morale or provided poor service to customers, unnecessary risks to take for someone who is not a good employee. If they are in a critical role, try to hold onto them until you can cover their responsibilities, then let them go. If the employee is a keeper, share that you heard they were considering leaving. Make an effort to understand their reasons, and make sure they have all of the information necessary to make such a big decision. You may know things about the company's future that they don't. Ask them to take some time to consider this newfound information; let them know you hope they decide to stay. If they are in the early stages of looking, you have an opportunity to convince them to give the company a chance. Retaining good employees is the payoff for playing "prevent defense."

6. Focus on the positive aspects of working at your company.

You are the company cheerleader and champion. This is what you are paid to do as a manager! Your job is not all customer service and overseeing projects; it's also about taking care of the company's most important asset — your people. Think of your employees as you would customers. Don't miss an opportunity to point out things like flexible hours, use of a company truck, recognition and reward, quality equipment, or a commitment to training and development that puts employees on track to higher level jobs. Keep a list of these benefits in your mind, ready to share at every opportunity. I am not suggesting that you teach your managers to walk around bragging to your employees about how great the company is, but subtle reminders can go a long way to improve employee retention.

> *West Texas, 105 degrees in the middle of a heatwave. I walked into the shop and leaned against the ice machine, saying out loud to no one in particular, "Saw a bunch of our competitor's employees buying ice at the gas station this morning." Our more experienced hands knew other*

companies made their employees pay for their own ice.
I patted the ice machine, suggesting one of our techs fill
his water cooler with "free" ice before he headed out into
the field for the day. I knew every time they took a cold
drink out there in the heat, they would be glad to have
plenty of "free" ice.

Teaching managers how to responsibly and respectfully handle employees is essential to growing a business into Stage Two. However, for a sustainable Stage Three business to operate on autopilot, you need to teach managers to think like owners. Having managers know how to make a profit, spend company money wisely and how to use basic principles on dealing with employees will pay off with a motivated workforce, and plenty of "free" time for yourself.

Opening Additional Offices

The ability to open additional offices is what allowed us to grow beyond a mom and pop service company into a significant regional competitor, large enough to attract private equity money. Many of our competitors tried and failed to open additional offices. So, what was our secret?

Franchises are able to do it by having in-house training and thick operational manuals that cover every aspect of a cloned string of operations and buildings. They also have central sourcing warehouses for supplies and products. Conceptually, Desert was similar in that we had an operations manual and we used the same vendors for most of our major purchases.

All of this sounds easy enough. So why is opening an additional office so challenging for a small business? It is difficult to find managers who can think like an owner — not just someone who wants to collect a paycheck for minimum effort. Unlike franchisees who have a financial stake in their offices, your company managers are dealing with *your* money, not their own.

We lost a lot of money finding a few honest, hardworking managers. There were plenty of employees who wanted the autonomy and perks of running an office, but lacked the responsibility that came with it. Some would say anything to land an arrangement that was good for them, even at the company's expense. Once you find the right manager to open a new office, give them the tools to support their efforts.

First, provide basic training in what will be expected on a daily, weekly, monthly, quarterly and yearly basis. The best training is completed on the job, under the watchful eye of another experienced manager. One priority of your existing managers should be to train their potential replacement.

This is good practice with or without opening additional offices. You never know when someone is going to quit or get poached by a competitor. My laziest manager was the best at training new managers. He saw the benefit in allowing someone else to do his work, acting more as a coach or supervisor.

In addition to training, we provided new managers with a lifeline. Managers could call the head operations manager any time they had a question. This was especially important while they were getting their feet wet and sharpening their decision-making skills. They established their own lifeline with fellow managers to discuss and compare their issues *before* "bothering the boss." An open line of communication is key. My operations manager spoke with each manager every day. As the owner, you should have regular, physical visits to each office to see what's *really* happening. Sometimes, we were amazed at what we found.

We aimed for a system of institutional learning. When an employee or a manager did something great we would have them write down what they did and how they did it. Smart ways of doing things were spread across the organization. We also kept lists of screw-ups to see if there was a pattern or particular situation where they were more likely to occur. The management would circulate these findings to every office as well, reminding them that screw-ups cost 10 times as much in revenue.

Building Better Bonuses

When I worked at Amoco, anytime we had a competitive exercise at a seminar or training, the managers would immediately try to circumvent the rules to their advantage. I was never surprised to learn that the first thing those managers did when the metrics for bonuses rolled out was try to game the system. When revenues and expenses were tracked by groups, some managers spent more time figuring out how to push expenses to other groups than trying to make a profit for the company. In other words, managers focused on accounting for metrics to get a bigger bonus instead of doing their actual job. Hard metrics are the defining factor in an institutional bonus system. I told myself I would figure out how to mitigate the tendency to try and manipulate the bonus game if I ever ran my own company.

Free Will: Best of Both Worlds

After selling Desert to the private equity firm, the MBAs reviewing the company initially laughed at the "Doug Frey Free Will Bonus Program." But when they saw how well it worked, they started to pay attention. My plan took the best of an institutional system and added a fluid component, creating a bonus program encouraging managers to focus on profit for the business and collaboration with their peers.

Bonuses were paid monthly as opposed to quarterly or annually because the short time between action and result motivated our managers who were used to being paid hourly. We used metrics to measure and reward revenue growth and profit. The fluid component was used to reward the little things a manager did to improve operations, revenue or profit for another office and the company at large. This simplified accounting and encouraged managers to work together for everyone's benefit.

A pure, institutional metric system often causes managers to become preoccupied on their own little island. In an effort to eliminate the island effect, big companies use metric systems that include a company-wide or regional metric. This seldom works in smaller companies or trade-based service businesses. The connection between a manager's individual efforts and effect on the company were just too vague. Also, the time frames for company-wide metrics were too long for folks that came from an hourly pay background.

When I gave metrics for bonuses based on revenue growth and profits, I showed the managers their growth and profit margins in percentages for comparison. Profits were shown as above or below company average for the month. The manager had to then explain deviation, in either direction, from average. This resulted in identifying and sharing best and worst practices company-wide. Metrics were shared with other managers and offices to engage our leaders competitively. Everyone wanted to come out on top.

The fluid system was not driven by hard metrics. This allows the owner to recognize and reward the managers' actions that generated revenue and profit for the whole company, especially when they helped out a fellow manager or office. The fluid system could consider things as simple as supplies lent to another office, or sending an extra set of hands from one office to another for a few days. Accounting for all of that on paper would have been overwhelming; the "free will" system let me take these things into account when awarding a bonus without wasting precious time tracking the small (but critical) stuff.

Occasionally, the "free will" bonus system let me take into account a manager's personal situation. If a key manager was in a financial bind, as nearly everyone is at some point, instead of giving them a loan or taking it out of a future bonus, I would bump up the timing of their bonus to cover their need. This built loyalty and helped keep good managers from leaving.

The Upside-Down Org Chart

I have always thought that organization charts with the boss at the top and the workers below didn't represent how organizations should work. **I think organization charts should show the boss underneath the workers, supporting them. After all, it is the primary job of the owner to make sure every employee has the tools, training, equipment, information *and* the will to do their job well.** People are mirrors — if your staff sees you as a service-oriented leader, it is likely they will reflect that style and provide quality service to the field staff, other employees and customers.

> *It was my last day at Desert. I looked around the office one more time. The bookshelves were empty and there were no pictures on the walls. My desk was cleared. Then, I spied them: my dirty, worn, steel-toed work boots. I learned many lessons about our business out in the field. I learned that to our customers, the service techs were our*

company. Seeing those work boots in my office reassured
our technicians that I understood and appreciated their
work. They sent a message to the entire company that
our techs, the folks engaging with our customers every
day — were the most vital people to our organization.

I also included the office staff below the field workers in our organizational chart. In my mind, the office staff was support staff. I found it common for employees in the office to think they were superior to the field hands. I always pointed out that our customers hired us for our field hands, not for our office staff. Anything we could do to make the field hands' job easier was an absolute necessity. Our office staff would move heaven and earth to make sure payroll was done on time and correctly. **Nothing is more important to an hourly employee than getting a paycheck on time.**

Human resources should accommodate the schedules of the hard-working employees providing services to your customers, not the other way around. This is especially important when HR-related paperwork must be submitted. Most companies require their employees to get paperwork to HR by a cut-off date. This can be particularly hard for personnel working out of town or in the field. Knowing that, we sent couriers to pick up their paperwork, which also motivated folks to complete it all on time. Sometimes we would combine paperwork with weekly operations like a safety meeting or invoice collection. Each one of our new hires would have to get used to this approach. Most organizations have their service employees (who are doing the work for the customers) also answering to the office staff, making their jobs even more difficult. It's best to have folks working directly with customers keep their focus there and not on internal matters.

The Office Staff Provides Customer Service, Too!

Taking care of the customer is everyone's job. Even though I made a point to remind employees that we were in business because of the service we provided, there was a strong emphasis on customer satisfaction. At Desert, we provided the field services of a big company with the personalized paperwork of a small one. If a customer wanted the invoice on pink paper, we would give them the invoice on pink paper. A lot of companies want the customer to accommodate *their* processes; I found it best to modify our processes to meet the customer's needs. Occasionally, we would get a disruptive or expensive (in time or money) request by a customer. In those cases, we would estimate the size and profitability of our work for them. If profit was high, we would gladly provide the extra service. If profit was tight, we would ask them to pay for us to provide the service, pointing out we were under a tight contract or pricing structure. We had surprising success in recouping costs where significant burdens were requested. More importantly, by tailoring our paperwork process to meet our customer needs, we made them "sticky" customers, meaning they wouldn't change to another service provider so easily. This is an important element to building a successful business. Someone looking to buy a company will pay extra for "sticky" customers, a key component of goodwill.

Growing Panes

When we bought the glass company, the previous owners had set up the business to compete on price. Profits were small, if there were any, and the phone didn't ring with repeat customers. Work was won by offering up the lowest price, and profit was made by haggling with the customer, often after the job was done. We turned this around by paying close attention to what was important to our customers. Several times our field techs worked through the night to get a building finished on time. Because we paid our vendors promptly, we were able to get materials faster than our competitors. This gave us an advantage on small but important rush jobs. We lost money on a few jobs at first, but we were learning and making a good investment in our future. It didn't take long for our new attitude to build a reputation in the business. After a couple of years, our phone was ringing with repeat customers and jobs with more profitable margins.

Sticky customers build goodwill! Make sure your managers understand this so they can make an environment where employees are able to provide the best service to your customers.

Invest in Your Managers

A manager's education is an ongoing process, not a singular event. The skills and knowledge required to be a good manager are completely different from those required of a good technician. Lead by example, because this will be their primary way of learning how you want things done. As your company grows, you will find that you can't be everywhere at once. Teach your managers to let company values steer their choices. Employees are usually promoted into management positions based on performance and personality. It's important to nurture that transition from employee to manager with training so that they realize their full potential and lead with confidence.

Definitions and Key Ideas

- **Delegation of authority:** a legal document that spells out the monetary and legal authority given to each manager.

- **Sticky customers:** a customer that will stay with you and continue to use your services even if competitors are cheaper. You create sticky customers by committing to accommodating their needs in ways that your competitors can't.

- **Upside-down org chart:** an organization chart that shows the boss underneath the workers, supporting them. After all, it is the primary job of the owner to make sure every employee has the tools, training, equipment, information and the will to do their job well.

- Train managers to think like owners.

- At Desert, we promoted our operating managers from the field ranks, which required expanding their skill set by teaching them how we operated financially. Try to grow your own.

- Taking care of the customer is everyone's job.

- Managers must take care of the company's most important assets: its people.

- Build a bonus system that rewards managers for doing what is best for the company.

8

Buying a Business

Everything in the book up to this point is focused on how you can improve on the business you already have. I pivot in this chapter, focusing on what to look for if you are in the market to purchase one. If you're not in the market for buying a business, I still suggest reading through this chapter so you can understand what buyers are looking for in the event that you might want to sell your business one day.

When most people think about small business owners, they probably imagine someone who started a company from scratch. Based on my experience as a manager at a big company, I knew I had the skill set to *run* a business, but I wasn't sure I had what it takes to *start* a business. So, I looked at buying a company where I saw potential for growth and profitability. But what kind of business?

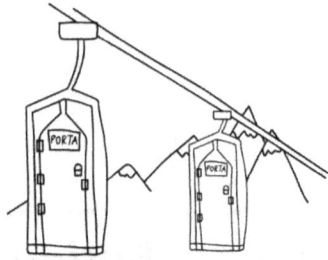

When I began to consider buying a business, one of my fishing buddies that owned a small company told me I had to be passionate about whatever I chose in order to be successful. I challenged him, doubting he was really passionate about his portable toilet business. I'm convinced he started his company to fit his ski-bum lifestyle. I pointed out that maybe it was his passion for skiing, not toilets, that inspired him to start his own business. The toilet company was a means to an end, but I think that's reason enough to go into business. **You don't have to be passionate about what your company does, but you need to be passionate about the business of business.**

I studied engineering at Texas A&M, but my real education started with my first employer, who spent a fortune training me in business. Their executive training program featured instructors from Harvard, Wharton, Princeton and Stanford — all the big-name schools. They introduced me to the work of Michael Porter, a professor at Harvard Business School. His article, "How Competitive Forces Shape Strategy," is among the most valuable tools I've come across. I recommend reading it before you buy or start a business. It taught me to evaluate the profitability potential of different businesses. Some lines of work are fundamentally more profitable than others (I prefer to avoid low-profit business). Porter's work taught me how to position a company to improve profitability and differentiate from competitors. To me, his article reinforces the idea that export-proof businesses have a lot of inherent advantages and potential to be profitable.

My mother always told me to never quit learning. Take my mother's advice and continue to read and study about business because it is ever-changing. I learned some very expensive lessons about small business over the years that cost much more than I spent on a college education.

Choosing the kind of business to pursue is as important as how you pursue it. Right off the bat, it's constrained by factors like available capital, your skill set and geographic location. Once you have a business in mind, ask yourself: How will you improve profitability and grow the company? Your answer should form the foundation of your business plan. Focus on what knowledge, skills and resources you will need.

Warning: I have condensed a tremendous amount of accounting, legal and financial concepts into a few very general guidelines. I am not an accountant or a lawyer, and my advice will always be to hire those professionals to walk you through your personal situation. However, this section should arm you with information to help steer discussions with your team of professionals.

Capital Considerations

If you are like I was and don't have much capital to purchase a business, consider trade-based service businesses. They don't usually have a lot of physical assets, so they are more affordable. Think about an electrician or a plumber: just about all they need is a truck and some hand tools. This is the reason service businesses are fundamentally less expensive to buy than asset-heavy businesses, like a manufacturing company.

When buying a business, **goodwill** is defined as certain intangible elements you will pay for that are difficult to measure. Some bankers call this "blue sky." Goodwill is also an accounting term for the difference between the value of hard assets you purchase and the price you pay for the company. A company name and associated reputation — factors that comprise the businesses goodwill — are often the most important items to consider when buying a small company.

Hard assets are those things a bank can take and sell if you are unable to pay your loan. Usually they are carried on the balance sheet as depreciating items. You want hard assets to help borrow money. Not having a lot of physical assets can be a liability when you want to borrow money to buy a business. Banks want hard assets to loan against, so buying a service company can require a lot of cash down (or high-cost debt). A business that is **asset light** does not have a lot of physical assets, so when a buyer is in the market to purchase one, they should pay more attention to sales history, performance and goodwill, as opposed to the equipment or tools.

On Goodwill & Buying or Selling

Often when purchasing service companies, the value of goodwill will often exceed the value of hard assets tied to the business. Sometimes buyers will focus on inspecting the smaller, physical assets because they are easier to measure; the bank requires it because these assets can be taken as collateral. Great care is taken in assessing the condition of vehicles and buildings, but too often little is done to inspect the goodwill portion of the purchase price. I made this mistake once and it was very costly. Since I don't have the opportunity to do that one over, I encourage you to learn about goodwill at my expense!

Sterling Partners, the private equity company who bought Desert, always makes a big effort to inspect and assess goodwill before they buy a company. For example, they require a senior deal manager to meet with several of a company's largest customers to quiz them about their experience and confirm the claims of the seller.

The Non-Disclosure Agreement

Once you have contacted someone about a business for sale, they normally require you to sign a **non-disclosure agreement**, or **NDA**, before providing any detailed information about the business. An NDA is a legal document that prohibits you from disclosing the information sent to you and prevents you from using that information to start a competing business. The agreement will often include a clause that prevents you from contacting any of the employees or vendors of the company, since such disclosure could significantly damage an ongoing business. Sometimes when employees find out a business is for sale, they will quit because they think the company is not financially sound or they are scared of change.

If your NDA is coming from a business broker, it will likely contain language that requires you to use that broker to buy the business and absolves the broker from liability regarding the accuracy of claims made about the business during the sale (specifically revenue, profitability and outlook). That liability waiver should be considered the first of many "buyer beware" signs one must pay attention to: It's up to you and your team of experts to verify everything.

Look Under the Hood

After signing the nondisclosure, you will be sent a **pitch book**, the memo and slides that discuss the business you are looking to purchase. It should contain basic accounting information including a current profit and loss statement, a balance sheet, historical profits and a high-level overview of the industry. Pitch books are written to make the business look great. Think of a real estate ad written to make a house sound attractive, pointing out the good features and completely overlooking any problems. There is frequent discussion of "owner's take," which is not the same as actual accounting profit; the accompanying financial statements are usually not prepared according to Generally Accepted Accounting Practice (GAAP) guidelines. Understanding the difference between owner's take and actual profit is critical in determining a fair price for the business (an explanation of these differences is included in the next section, "Negotiating Price.")

After reading the pitch book, begin your due diligence process. Check things out online. How does the business fare on sites that offer customer reviews? Review their web presence. Are the photos featured in their pitch book and website outdated? Research competitors in the area. How does your desired company stack up?

Next, visit the business and meet the owners. Does what you see match what you were told? Is the equipment new and well-kept? Is the shop clean? I have always thought I could tell how good a tech was by how clean they kept their pickup truck. A business is no different. An unkempt, messy shop is likely to house a business with poorly managed records, unrefined processes and poorly maintained employees.

People interested in buying a business are always looking for the owner who's looking to retire, leaving behind a great business with predictable recurring net income. In other words, buyers are searching for a unicorn.

Keep asking questions. If it's a really good business, why would they sell? And if they are selling what do they know that you do not? You should be comfortable with answers to questions like these before spending time and a significant amount of money on **due diligence**. If your gut makes you suspicious, do not ignore the warning signs. Spend most of your time on this initial check, making a personal assessment of the sellers. Are they trustworthy?

Due diligence is the research and analysis of an organization done in preparation for a business transaction.

Do inventory and supplies seem consistent with the level of sales in the financial statements? Go through each line of the profit and loss statement and the balance sheet. Ask questions about every category to make sure you understand what it is and how it affects the business. All major revenues, expenses and assets should be investigated in great detail during due diligence. Proceed with caution! The seller always knows more than the buyer!

Multiple of Earnings

What is the right multiple of earnings to pay for a company? There are many factors that affect the earnings multiple, but quality of earnings (predictability) is the largest. This predictability, or risk of earnings, is dependent on: organizational capacity, market share, brand name, quality of product or service, uniqueness of product and barriers to competitors. These are things that the owner can and should influence or manage. The outlook for the business in general also controls the multiple.

Negotiating Price

One of the most stunning things I have learned about business acquisition is that **most small service businesses sell for between three and five times their net earnings.** This is in sharp contrast to the price to earnings ratio (PE ratio) found on Wall Street. Even slow-growth companies, like those who sell consumer products or automakers, typically sell in the upper single digits. Companies with average growth prospects can sell at PE ratios of 12 to 20, and multiples of 30 to 100 are possible for some high-growth tech companies. The Wall Street average is about 15 to 20 times earnings, which is why so many small business owners dream of capitalizing on their hard work and taking their company public with an IPO (initial public offering).

Net earnings in this section are defined as **EBITDA**, an accounting term that stands for Earnings Before Interest, Taxes, Depreciation and Amortization. To get the EBITDA of a company, take the profit (net income) then add interest paid, taxes paid, the depreciation and amortization.

EBITDA = PROFIT + INTEREST PAID + TAXES + DEPRECIATION + AMORTIZATION

Warning! Small business brokers may try to confuse you about net earning. They might talk about the owner's total "take" and add things to earnings like the owner's salary, relatives' salaries (usually the spouse and often their adult children), vehicles for family use, etc. This is done in an attempt to increase the price you will pay for the business. The broker's commission is tied to the sales price. It's in the seller's (and the broker's, but not *your*) best interest to talk up the value of the business.

Determining the actual owner's take is called **recasting the books.** Listen to your broker's reasons for including the items in net income, but discuss each one with your banker, lawyer and accountant. This is a common area of disagreement between the buyer and seller.

As the buyer, think of buying the business as an ongoing concern. If you have to work in the business or hire someone to work in it, then the money and benefits paid to the owner are not earnings for the company, but wages for the owner's effort. These wages should not be included in earnings when calculating the value of a business.

You will need to think about these "add-backs" to determine if they should be included in the earnings. If you have to shoulder the expenses to make the revenue, they are expenses, not "owner's take," profit or earnings.

Conversely, there may be expenses that do not affect the ability to generate revenue. These are potential add-backs to the profit. For example, if the owner's kid, now away in college, is using a company truck as a personal vehicle, then it should be "added back" to profits because the expense of that truck is essentially profit taken as a truck instead of cash. The new owner may decide to get rid of the truck, making the eliminated truck part of additional cash profit.

If you buy a small business where the only money "profit" is what the owner is paid after expenses, you are not buying a profitable company — you are buying yourself a paycheck. **A company should only be deemed profitable after the expense of paying the owner's fair market salary is deducted from net income for the business.**

Recasting the books magnifies any error, so accurately accounting for these items is very important. Each dollar difference in earnings affects the sales price by the multiple of the earnings. Remember, service businesses tend to sell for three to five times their net earnings.

Low vs. High Multiples

The construction industry is generally at the low end of the range (maybe a two or three multiple) because of the low barriers to entry (meaning it's easy to get into) and the cyclical nature of the business. Bankers know that many construction businesses are started during housing booms and are all-too familiar with auctioning construction equipment during a housing bust. On the other end of the spectrum, online software companies are valued at a 40 or 50 multiple of earnings. Those providers (Adobe, Quickbooks, Dropbox, etc.) have a lot of subscribers; and if they lose a few there is minimal effect on earnings. Customers are not likely to drop service once they subscribe because they would have to build new processes and learn new software. Bankers and business buyers love predictability, recurring revenue and profits, which is why companies with predictable earnings bring high multiples.

Unlike the stock market, high growth rates don't necessarily result in higher multiples for small companies. Generally, buyers love to see high growth rates motivating them to buy the company. But high growth rates seldom result in significantly higher multiples. Knowing that, don't fall for a company's growth story and overpay for the business. Value the company based on actual earnings over the past 12 months (called **trailing twelve months, or TTM**). The experts at buying are very disciplined at not overvaluing and overpaying. Follow their lead to avoid a financial disaster.

Based on my experience, don't plan on taking home a lot of money right after you buy a business, even if it is very profitable. Upfront, you have to pay the bank-note and all the things you missed when you evaluated the business initially, not to mention the money you have to put in for prospective growth. In my experience, it generally takes two to three years after buying a business before you can expect any money (above a salary commensurate with my efforts) to come of it.

The LOI

The Letter of Intent (LOI) is the first legal document that says, "I want to buy your business." It generally states the price, what you are buying, time frame and the terms the deal is subject to, which will decide the final price and timing of the deal.

The price is your best guess at valuation of the business after looking under the hood. Final price is dependent on the results of due diligence, where your team of experts (legal, accounting and banking) all look at the business and assets represented by the seller. Normally, the pitch book, along with balance sheets and a preliminary analysis (including the actual financial P&L statement) will be disclosed by the seller. The two parties come up with an agreed price that will be written in the LOI. The letter usually contains language stating the deal is dependent on everything checking out consistent with what has been disclosed by the seller. If the buyer finds something significant during due diligence that was not previously disclosed, the legal framework is there to adjust the price. The buyer should not re-trade the deal after the LOI has been written unless there is a good reason found while performing due diligence. If the buyer tries to re-trade the deal without a really good reason, beware!

Your time frame will be driven by how long it will take to arrange financing (think about closing on a home and waiting on the mortgage) and due diligence. These items will comprise your LOI.

Due Diligence

The bank will make sure you thoroughly analyze the value of the hard assets when you do your due diligence. The hard part is making sure what you are buying is all there. When private equity firms buy a company, they hire high-powered accounting firms to do a "quality of earnings analysis," which requires the firm to completely redo several years of the company's books to make sure all expenses, inventory and revenues were handled properly and the profit is really there. This is a considerable expense and not cost effective for a small business. You can do a similar check for less money by looking closely at a sampling of data in several critical categories. Thorough due diligence can save you from making a huge financial mistake and inheriting big headaches down the road.

Sellers have been caught manipulating their accounting system by including fake invoices to increase their accounts receivable and paper profits. Your CPA should send a letter to several of the seller's customers and have them match their bills from the company with what their records show as "sent." I always have my CPA get copies of the business's checking account records directly from the bank. It takes some time, but an accountant can plug in all the expenses and investments for a period of time and duplicate what the books should show. Any discrepancy between these two items and there had better be a good explanation!

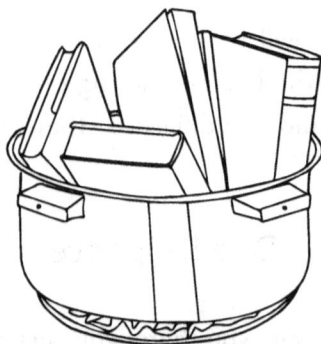

Several sellers have been reluctant to let me take a closer look at their financials because they were "cooking the books" for income tax reasons. It's not uncommon for people to push some gray area personal expenses through the company. Beware! If they would steal from the government, even with the penalties for tax evasion, why would they hesitate to mislead you? I always request copies of the owner's income taxes to make sure they match the company books. No one is going to report *more* than they are making, so it's good to double-check. The government has severe penalties for tax evasion, so this is a good way to truth-test the company books.

I also look for the involvement of a third party in their account-ing process. Do they have annual audits or compiled financial statements done by a CPA? If they have a bank loan, it's common for banks to require annual financial statements prepared by an accounting firm. I like when there is a bank involved. Conversely, I see red flags when company operations are run by one member of a married couple and the books are handled by the other.

Goodwill should be reviewed every bit as closely as hard assets. Go see the customers, preferably without the owner (if the owner will not allow this, that's another big red flag). Ask them: How is the company's service? Are there areas for improvement?

Has the owner ever lied or cheated them? Do they have a lot of repeat customers and long-term business?

Do they have a large number of clients or just a few that account for most of their revenue? If it's just a few heavy hitters, what are the chances they would continue as customers with new ownership? Having only a few big customers (one is the worst case) is known as "the risk of customer concentration." Ask these questions up front and take their answers into consideration; any issues will impact the price. The list of questions evaluating goodwill could go on, but your accountant and lawyer should be able to identify what you need to know for the business you are considering and investigate accordingly.

If your accountant and your lawyer are unfamiliar with the value and importance of goodwill, you must find someone with experience in that area. Don't let the professionals you are paying learn on your dime: expect them to be expert. The money up front may seem like a lot, but hiring experienced professionals can prevent very expensive mistakes. Lawyers will often steer their clients toward purchasing the assets (physical and intangible) of the company and not buying the entire company. If you buy a company, not just the assets, you assume the liability for any work done prior to you owning the business. It's nearly impossible to determine the potential of this liability.

Your lawyer will want you to understand if any work contracts are assumable, which means they can be reassigned to the new owner. This is particularly important with Master Service Agreements (MSA's), which are the basic legal framework for service work that is done repeatedly for the same customer. They eliminate the need for a new contract each time the service is provided, making an MSA harder to obtain from major customers.

Evaluating contracts like these is a ton of work, but there is a lot of money at stake.

Once you have looked under the hood and understand what you are going to buy, the next step is figuring out how you are going to pay for the deal.

Financing the Dream

My dad managed a grocery store for 30 years, but he always dreamed of owning one. He was great with people: customers liked him; he did a good job of managing the large number of hourly employees. He loved marketing. He certainly had all the experience and tools to run a store. However, finance was not his thing. I will never forget my Mom telling me that they just couldn't figure out the money part to owning their own store. Understanding financing is probably the biggest hurdle in transitioning from paycheck to business owner.

Of all the questions I have received over the years about owning a business, how to buy one and finance it is the greatest mystery. Our general reluctance to ask details about someone else's personal finances certainly stymies discussion on the topic and few financial professionals write about it because it is complicated and ever-changing.

New businesses are often financed on savings as well as loans from friends, family and credit card companies. If you think you may want to start a business one day, putting all of your savings into a 401K plan can be a trap. Financial advisors often tell you to put all of your savings into these plans. But why put your money where you pay a penalty to use it before retirement?

Obtaining a Loan

The solution to financing the purchase of a business often involves using a bank. Most people do not have a financial relationship with a bank beyond a personal checking or savings account, so approaching the bank for a business loan can be intimidating. For what it's worth, when you start working on a business loan, your relationship with the bank will be elevated considerably.

The notion that banks only give loans to people who don't need one is common. Think getting a home mortgage is tough? It is the simplest and easiest loan to obtain because it is "covered" by the house and your history of payment is readily available. The bank has much more to consider for business loans: the evaluation of physical assets and intangible assets; your ability to run the business and finally, the outlook for the business.

Let's start with the physical or "hard" assets. The bank will require you to hire and pay for a CPA firm to audit the equipment on the depreciation table that goes into the company's balance sheet. A **depreciation table** shows how the accountants determine the current value of the equipment shown on the balance sheet. Each type of equipment has a useful life (how long accountants say it will be usable). Then, they will reduce the value of the equipment to reflect how much life is left in it. Accounting life and actual life of a physical asset can vary dramatically. Equipment worth is considerably different than what is shown on the balance sheet. The bank will require you to bring in experts to determine the actual current value of the physical assets, particularly for any specialized industrial equipment. For example, most cars and light trucks are fully depreciated in five years, so they have no value on the balance sheet if they are five years old or older. But if you take care of a truck, it can be useful for much more than five years. I ran into the opposite case. The trucks still had value on the balance sheet, but they were total junkers in real life. I had to replace almost the whole fleet in the first few years I owned the company. This was a big expense I wasn't expecting. I had done a poor job of due diligence on that item and it was a very expensive lesson!

One important category to assess in many service companies is the value of the trucks and other vehicles. A vehicle's value will be assessed using the Kelly Blue Book or another guide. Then, the bank will discount that number to account for the cost of their effort to sell it. You are essentially getting multiple loans for used vehicles. The interest rate is typically high, and the value of the vehicles is greatly discounted. Even with the discount, vehicles are one of the most valued assets to the bank because there is a ready market for them and they are mobile. Office furniture and industrial equipment are of lesser value. For example, used office furniture is often sold by the pound in big quantities. A company may deem these items of great value on the books, but to a bank, they are priced and valued as they would be at an auction or garage sale.

The value of these hard assets is the basis for most bank loans to small businesses. These loans against assets are called **senior debt** because the bank will hold a lien against all of these assets. If you go out of business, the bank will sell these assets to cover their loan.

I actively sought out companies going out of business who were selling their equipment for pennies on the dollar. Buying used equipment allowed us to ramp up our size on a tight budget. New employees would see that management had basic, functional furniture and realize it was part of our culture.

For a small company, it is very difficult to get financing for intangible assets. Many banks will not loan against intangible assets (goodwill, intellectual property or other "blue sky") for a new operator, so you have to come up with this money yourself. If they do loan against intangible assets, expect to pay a very high interest rate on this money. Charging high interest rates is how banks justify the risk of loaning against assets that are hard to value and sell.

The bank will require you to sign a personal guarantee that pledges your personal assets as collateral for a loan. This is risky: The bank has little sympathy if things go wrong and they have to sell your personal assets. Even if the company has more than enough hard assets to cover the loan, the bank will often ask for your personal guarantee as well.

Banks like to have double or triple coverage on their loan amount. Technically, signing a personal guarantee is negotiable, but they are the ones with the money and as they say, "He who has the gold makes the rules." A loan officer at the bank will require you to submit a personal financial statement, which is a balance sheet for *you*. It will list all of your assets: bank accounts, stock accounts, your house, cars and any personal items of significant value (guns, jewelry, etc.). Then you will list any outstanding debts or loans: student loans, car loans, etc. The bank will want a complete picture of your personal finances, verification of income and proof of payments: monthly checking, house payments, auto loan payments, club membership fees — you get the idea. And yes, they will want to look at several years of personal tax returns. I call this the financial colonoscopy.

When you look at buying an existing business, the two major components are physical assets and goodwill. Intangible assets of the company — intellectual property, brand name, customer loyalty to the company and organizational capability all fall under goodwill.

To the banker, goodwill is viewed as the ability of the company to continue making a profit. Chief among their concerns are: Will the new owner continue, much less improve, the profitability and operations of the company? A track record of running a business is very valuable in this assessment. This is another reason why it's more difficult for someone to transition from a paycheck job to buying or owning a company.

Happy Birthday

It was my 50th birthday and I was paying our bills like I did every Wednesday. I noticed that we only had a few months left on the loan we had taken out to buy the company. I walked into the bank and handed our banker the payoff amount on our note. We finally owned our business after nearly six, very long years. As I left the building, I felt a huge burden had been lifted from me; the best birthday gift I could imagine. I drove home listening to Dave Ramsey, shouting at the top of my lungs every time someone would call in and yell, "I'm debt free!" I'm sure I looked like an idiot to those driving by but I didn't care. I was happy!

Financing Your Operations: The Line of Credit

Banks know that once you've bought a company and begin operating, you will need money for operations. They will often include a **line of credit (LOC)** along with your loan package to purchase the business. This is the easiest time to obtain one since the bank already has all of the financial data on you and the business. The bank evaluates an LOC by assessing the quality of your accounts receivable (i.e., will you really get paid and when), then sets a rate of interest based on their estimate of the risk of your company getting paid. There are also plenty of non-bank lenders out there that lend against receivables, so check their rates and service to compare against what a bank could provide with an LOC.

Why do you need a Line of Credit? Once you start running your new business, you will find that all your earnings are "locked up" in accounts receivable — products or services that you have billed out but customers have not paid for yet. While waiting on payment, you still have payroll, bills to pay, inventory to purchase, rent, utilities and at the end of it all, yourself. Expect to start with a small LOC that can increase with your business as the bank gains confidence in the company. A line of credit with a bank will make it easier to grow.

Purchase Agreement

Start with a middle-of-the-road purchase agreement or you will spend a fortune in legal fees finding middle ground. If your lawyer doesn't know what middle ground is in a transaction, you need a new lawyer. A good test for this balanced starting point is to look at something simple. If it is straightforward and reasonable, you are probably in a good place. If you need to negotiate on a simple item, you can bet the more complicated stuff will be just as one-sided. I have seen big law firms intentionally start with obvious, one-sided agreements in an effort to run up a tab on the seller *and* the buyer. Do not tolerate this. Ask for a new starting document and/or a new law firm if either side opens with a one-sided agreement. Let your lawyer and their lawyer make the effort to change documents as necessary.

It's important to know the value of your hard assets, but you should be focused on the valuation of the non-physical assets: goodwill, badwill, intellectual property, customer lists and contact information, liabilities, disgruntled customers or employees — any source of a potential legal issue.

One of the best legal minds I've ever worked with has always said that **the most important sections in a purchase agreement are the representations and warranties**. This section can protect you from lawsuits and liabilities that are impossible to identify by going through a seller's books and records. It can also be helpful if you later discover fraud. Most importantly, it shifts your due diligence liability from anything missed as your loss to the seller's liability to properly disclose everything. This is a very important legal point. If the seller will not sign this section without a lot of negotiating, consider this a red flag, maybe even a deal breaker.

When we bought the glass company, I let my ego get the best of me and it cost us a lot of money. I didn't use a banker, so didn't have a second set of eyes — big mistake. I always use a banker when I do a land or building purchase because they have real expertise in these types of transactions. With the glass company, there was no land or building; the physical assets were not very significant.

Nevertheless, I should have included a banker just to have a second set of eyes. Although I used my law firm, they put a junior lawyer on it since the deal was small. We missed several things that in retrospect should have been red flags. Fortunately, it turned out okay, but there were a few really rough years that we lost money and had to work like crazy to overcome our mistakes. It would have been a lot easier if we had caught the red flags in the beginning. There will always be things you miss when you buy a company. Use all your resources and hope anything you miss ends up being small!

Managing Change After a Buyout

If you buy a company or become a partner in one, you will be starting in an environment of change and trepidation. Managing those feelings should be a priority. When someone's job, title and income are uncertain, people are immediately on edge. They imagine their whole world is at risk when their paycheck is threatened: where they live, what they eat, their children's future. Do not let this strain continue or people will quit.

During a buyout, have a meeting with all the employees as quickly as possible. Tell them about your family or share something personal; show them you are a real person, not some ogre coming to replace them with strangers. Assure your new employees that their jobs are safe. If there are major changes, be thoughtful about the way you explain them. Point out that if illegal or unsafe practices are found, they will be changed immediately. Reassure your new employees that while changes will occur over time, you intend to include employees in the decision-making process.

Including impacted people yields the best solutions and reduces fear of change.

My final point was always: "Just tell me." I could not solve problems I didn't know about. The last thing I wanted was for people to quit without sharing their issues, without giving me a fair shot at fixing them. This was the crux of my speech when I bought several different companies. It is important to include everyone involved in some way, and face to face is always best. This will improve the acceptance and success of the new company.

Buying a business will require you to do many new things that are complicated: legal agreements, accounting, asset evaluation and dealing with bankers. Do not be intimidated by this process. No one knows how to do all of these things. Buying or starting a business is where you develop relationships with lawyers, accountants and bankers who will become your trusted, professional advisors. Hopefully, they will be with you for the long haul as your company grows and everyone prospers!

Definitions and Key Ideas

- **Add-backs:** items in the current owner's expense such as a vehicle, which the new owners could elect convert to additional net income.

- **Amortization:** similar to depreciation, except it's the value of non-physical assets like goodwill. These are written down over time on company books. In terms of tax accounting, goodwill is normally amortized over 15 years.

- **Asset light:** a business with few physical assets. These businesses are marketing to buyers based on their sales history, performance and goodwill, as opposed to the equipment or tools they own.

- **Depreciation:** the loss in value of a physical asset over a specific period of time as recorded by an accountant.

- **Depreciation table:** a table that illustrates how the accountants determine the current value of old or worn equipment shown on the balance sheet.

- **Depreciation value:** the accountant's value of a physical asset over time as it wears out.

- **Due diligence:** the research and analysis of a company or organization done in preparation for buying or selling a business.

- **Earnings multiple:** how many times the earnings are multiplied to determine the price offered or paid for a business.

- **EBITDA:** earnings before interest, tax, depreciation and amortization.

- **Generally Accepted Accounting Practice (GAAP):** the set of accounting practices and principles that are accepted as the standard in America.

Definitions and Key Ideas (continued)

- **Hard assets:** physical items a bank can take and sell if you are unable to pay your loan.

- **Letter of intent (LOI):** the first legal document that says, "I will buy your business;" includes a starting price for the company.

- **Net earnings:** (EBITDA) = profit + interest paid + taxes + depreciation + amortization

- **Non-bank lenders:** Financial institutions that are not legally regulated as banks because they do not offer both lending and depositing services. Nonbanks often engage in "factoring" receivables (lending money against accounts receivable as collateral). They may also provide credit card processing and other lending services.

- **Non-disclosure agreement (NDA):** a legal document where you promise not to disclose the information sent to you. In business context, it also prevents you from competing against the one you are looking to buy.

- **Pitch book:** the memo and slides that discuss the business you are looking to purchase.

- **Profit and loss (P&L) statement:** a financial statement that summarizes the revenues, costs and expenses a business incurs during a specific period of time — usually a month, fiscal quarter or year.

- **Quality of earnings analysis, or recasting the books:** the process of completely redoing several years of a company's books to make sure all expenses, inventory and revenues were handled properly and the profit is really there.

Definitions and Key Ideas (continued)

- **Senior debt:** a lender's loans against the borrower's assets. The bank will hold a lien against all these assets. If anything happens and you go out of business, the bank will sell these assets to cover their loan.

- **Trailing twelve months (TTM):** the EBITDA for the company over the past 12 months.

- **Valuation:** what you or the owner thinks the company is worth, usually stated as a multiple of earnings.

- Figuring out financing is probably the biggest hurdle in transitioning from paycheck to business owner.

- You don't have to be passionate about what your company does, but you need to be passionate about the business of business.

- When purchasing service companies, the value of goodwill will often far exceed the value of hard assets tied to the business.

- Company profits are what is left after paying the owner's fair market salary. If all the profits of the company are taken as pay and they are merely a fair price for the owner's work, you aren't buying a business, you are buying a paycheck.

- The most important sections in a purchase agreement are the representations and warranties.

- Never quit learning, especially from the experience of others. Business lessons are extremely expensive!

9

Selling Your Business

This section is included because you need to start with the end in mind. Not everyone wants to leave a business to family. Some people sell because they feel burned out, want to retire, take life slower or they have other things they would rather do. None of these applied in my case but they often play a large role in the decision for others. If you have put in the time and effort to grow your business to Stage Two or Three, it will likely be worth something if you decide to sell.

In my case, we didn't have any family members that wanted to step in and run the company, so the private equity approach was attractive. It allowed us to take a meaningful amount of money out of the company by selling 70 percent to a private equity firm. We would still be in the game if the oil patch continued to boom by keeping the remaining 30 percent.

My partner and I made the decision to sell Desert, even though it was doing really well. We understood the risk in having all of our eggs in one basket. I knew several folks that had everything tied up in Enron and lost it all. While Desert wasn't run like Enron, I wanted to avoid having most of my personal wealth tied up in one company, even if I was the one running it. When we decided to sell Desert, it was by far the single largest asset for my partner and me.

> **Lord ONE MORE BOOM I PROMISE NOT TO PISS IT AWAY**

We had been in the oil business for about 40 years, enough to see booms and busts. Our industry was thriving, but it wouldn't take much of a downturn for Desert to lose most of its value. At the age of nearly 60, I was concerned about being able to live long enough for things to come back. There was a famous bumper sticker in the oil patch that said, "Lord, one more oil boom. I promise not to piss it away," which summarized our thinking on boom/bust cycles. Desert was well into Stage Three and could run without me being there every day, but we had too much at risk if the oil business went bust, so selling seemed like the right choice.

There are a number of ways to go about selling, and most are tied to the size of your business. If your business is small — under $10 million in net income — the most common approach is to sell to another person or group of people.

A business broker can help sell your business. If you go that route, exercise the same care in selecting a broker as you would a realtor: you will now be on the other side of the table discussed in the last chapter on "Buying a Business." In any case, have a trusted lawyer and accountant guide you through this process. Include all of your advisors. (I certainly included my wife who has helped me through a lot of big changes over the years). It is always a good idea to have a second pair of eyes.

Private Equity

Private equity (PE) firms buy the majority of mid-market businesses (those with over $10 million in EBITDA) in America today. They are called private equity partners because they usually only buy a portion of the business, almost always a majority stake of over 50 percent, usually 60 to 70 percent. They manage the risk of the purchase by requiring the previous owner to retain the remaining stake in the business. This arrangement allows the owner to take some chips off the table while still helping with the transition and continuation of the business. Selling a business smaller than middle market is difficult because it's less likely that someone has the money to purchase it (quite evident in the section of this book titled, "Financing the Dream"). PE firms typically buy companies, fix them up, grow them and resell them. Think of these firms like the folks who flip houses, but on a much larger scale. Their most common tactic for growth is to buy other companies that do the same thing and "bolt them on." This yields economies of scale and eliminates significant administrative staff. PE firms do these bolt-on acquisitions using money from investors and loans for leverage. How and when to use these loans is known as financial engineering. The leverage greatly increases the rate of return on the capital investment.

Owners of PE firms make money by charging fees and holding/ obtaining interest in each company purchased. They create value by growing the business, which is attractive because larger companies have more predictable earnings and higher purchase price multiples. For example, a lower, middle market company with $10 million in earnings might get a four multiple of EBITDA when purchased, but after a PE firm buys it and grows its earnings to $50 million, they can sell for an eight multiple. Therefore, the value of the company goes from $40 million to $400 million! Imagine if the next buyer doubles earnings to $100 million and takes it public at a sixteen multiple — now the company is worth $1.6 billion. I hope that motivates you to build your company as much as possible and keep the increase in multiple for yourself!

Many of the suggestions in this book are straight out of the private equity playbook on how to grow a company. **Private equity firms are a good example of the opportunities available when you work on your company instead of in the company.** At some level of revenue and net income, it makes sense to bring in outside help. The level that is right for you will depend on your risk tolerance, personal knowledge and ability, and that of your accounting, banking and legal advisors. When we began the process of selling Desert, I sought out a PE firm as a first step in the sales process because we wanted to take some, but not all, of our chips off the table. We also wanted access to their knowledge and their expertise at selling, as well as their knowledge of financial engineering to acquire additional bolt-on companies. We believed that selling to a private equity firm was in the best long-term interest of our employees. Being part of a bigger company would give them more career running room and better benefits than we were able to offer.

Picking a Private Equity Partner

There are some basic things to consider when selecting a PE firm. Primarily, you should consider what they're worth, how long they have been in business, what their financial track record is and how much will they be willing to pay. If you use a broker, they will often push you toward making a selection based on price (since they collect a fee based on sales price) and will justify it by saying something like: "All PE firms are the same. They can all do the job." I believe that the fit with you and your culture is more important than price. But determining if the fit is there is much more complicated.

What you see is what you get. When we decided to bring the PE firm Sterling Partners into Desert, I thought about the guidelines I used to choose my spouse and my business partner. How could I apply our Four F's to picking a private equity firm? When we first met, it was important to establish a shared set of values in order to have a harmonious working relationship. Shared values were more important to us than money. We ended up taking Sterling's

offer, which was several million dollars less than the other offers
we had received. Over the next few months, I struggled, wonder-
ing if we made the right decision. Sterling had a successful track
record and the faith and confidence of institutional investors, but
we literally gave up millions of dollars. However, when I visited
their office, they confirmed what they had assured us. Seeing their
workspace proved they had friendly, easy working relationships
with one another, which had not been the case when I visited
other financial firms that were hyper-competitive. At Sterling, the
senior management was interested in continuously training staff
in the latest business theories and ideas. I could tell they invested
in their employees by the shelf full of newly released business
books next to the break room.

> At dinner, I had the opportunity to meet two of the
> founding partners at Sterling. One perused the wine list
> for quite some time after asking my preference. Other
> private equity firms tended to order the most expensive
> bottle to impress me. After a few awkward minutes, I
> asked if I could help him decide. He replied, "I am looking
> for the best value wine that will also be to your liking."
> That impressed me. I have gone to great lengths to teach
> that principle of good value to our managers. The waiter
> took our order for appetizers and the perfect bottle of
> wine. When the appetizers showed up it was clear the
> waiter had taken advantage of the situation and upsold
> us excessively on food we didn't order. I overheard the
> other partner instruct one of his assistants to alert the
> manager to adjust the bill. What the waiter did wasn't
> right and it wasn't an issue of money. Sterling could

certainly afford it, but because of their principles, they would not tolerate it. I like dealing with principled people: You know what to expect and how they will act. Sterling lived up to everything they promised and were very careful not to overstate their capabilities in our dealings with them.

Were we right to select a partner based on values and not the highest bid? Absolutely! Our ability to work with Sterling resulted in a high level of mutual respect and was critical to our success. Sterling was involved for a little over two years, which is a very short hold period for a PE firm. They took notice and paid attention when we suggested selling while the oil market was still high. We ended up closing our sale to a public company literally weeks before the oil market crashed. That key decision, which was based on mutual respect, made the sale a home run for both of us.

Life After Sell Off

Did you really just decide to lay yourself off? The decision to sell your business is not easy and it can be much more difficult than the decision to start one. Knowing that selling also means big changes for everyone at the company can weigh heavy on an owner. Employees can become part of an extended family, and some of them may also be good friends. Selling is like a giant divorce with multiple parties. The people you have seen on a regular basis for years will no longer be part of your daily life. For me, the decision to sell was mentally like dealing with death or being laid off. A friend of mine knows a lot of entrepreneurs who have sold their businesses. He says to count on two years of depression after you sell. Selling Desert was one of the hardest things I have ever done. As you start to think about selling, start making a plan for life after the sale.

A lot of folks get so caught up in the sale of the business that they have no plan for themselves after it's said and done. You can be set adrift in life when you sell your business. Work is how most people, especially business owners, define themselves. You have been going to work every day for years; now, you will start to lose your connection with the people there on a daily basis.

So, if you plan to sell, make sure you have a plan for life after the sale, too. Build an after-business plan with just as much effort and care as you did your actual business plan. Just as you need professional help running your business, I suggest seeking professional help with life after business. Your world will change in a big way when you sell — make sure you are getting the exercise you need and the medical checkup appropriate for your age. And don't be too proud to see a therapist. You will likely have a lot to talk about! Well-meaning spouses, partners, family and friends often don't have the skills to help figure out how to fill the void that you may experience after you sell your business.

Some folks, like me, will discover they are "serial entrepreneurs," eager to start another business after a short break to catch their breath. Many realize this before the sale and start a new one before they sell their existing business. Others turn to the nonprofit world. With a pile of money, they can turn their considerable talents to activities that generate a huge return for the heart. The world benefits from the folks that take this route. The key to life post-sale is to stay healthy and active. Enjoy your success and share it with the people and organizations you think are important.

This is a book about growing and buying a business, but if you succeed on those two, you may very well want to sell it. Start with the end in mind!

Definitions and Key Ideas

• **Financial engineering:** how and when to use money from investors and loans for leverage.

• **Private Equity (PE) firms:** the organizations that buy the majority of mid-market businesses (those with over $10 million in EBITDA) in America today. They are called private equity partners because they usually only buy a portion of the business — almost always a majority stake of over 50 percent, usually about 60 or 70 percent.

• Were we right to select a private equity partner based on values and not the highest bid? Absolutely! Find partners that align with your values.

• Start with the end in mind and have a plan for life after sell-off! Stay healthy and active.

Conclusion

In the end, the comfort of a steady paycheck often beats the greater opportunity of starting your own business. You have to overcome the fear of the unknown to take the leap. And you should look before you leap. Have a plan; investigate the business you want and understand the economic drivers. Look under the hood and dig into the details like crazy — your profits are in the detail. Do your homework. This is the bet of a lifetime. The purpose of this book is to give you the insight and confidence to make good on that bet.

We are fortunate to live in the greatest country in the world. America's unique combination of democracy and capitalism has resulted in unmatched innovation and created the world's greatest economy. In recent times, we have developed the microchip, personal computers, the smart phone, the internet, Amazon, Google, Facebook and Uber. Hidden quietly behind these big marquee names are our country's millions of small businesses that provide ordinary and everyday **export-proof** services like yard work, painting, pool cleaning, plumbing, electrical work and many others. Business to business opportunities are even bigger. Our glass company is a good example of how a basic service can be scaled to multimillion dollar size for jobs that have to be done on-site. Exporting them is impossible. Fact is, the owners of many simple service businesses are millionaires. That is the great American story I know and love. This country is fertile ground for the ambitious and the risk takers. You have the opportunity to create a wonderful life for yourself and others. Go get your piece of the American pie!

Acknowledgments

My work family at Desert deserves credit for most of the examples in this book. In particular, I'd like to thank the technicians who have contributed so much to my blue collar education and my success. They are the real heroes in a service business.

Elic Brymer, my operations manager, taught me invaluable lessons about how service techs think about their job and the struggles they face. I considered him my partner at Desert, even if that was not our legal arrangement. Many of the lessons about operations in this book came from him. Kristin Bennett ran the office at Desert. She started as a bookkeeper and was eventually promoted to VP of Finance as the company grew. She did much to give me a practical education in the stages of a company while we were dealing with crazy levels of growth.

Mackenzie Smith deserves credit for encouraging me to actually write the book that has always been in me. As an editor, project manager and creative consultant, she polished my worn-out stories and ideas into a book. Her steady questioning of the details of business has made the book a useful tool for people who want to run a trade-based business. She has a rare talent to be engaging and challenging at the same time to bring out the best in folks. Even during the dark days (and nights) of editing, she kept the mood lively. It would have been easy to get bogged down and give up on the project a dozen times if she hadn't kept the dream alive. Mackenzie is incredibly talented and a very special person. I am lucky she agreed to work with me on this book.

Much credit is also due to her team: Jason Kelley, who designed the layout and cover of the book; Stacy Antoville for the illustrations; James Barch for copy editing in the beginning; Joshua Bennett Winer for editing toward the end of the project; and Dylan Owens for proofreading. Mackenzie provided the spark that has made "Export Proof" more entertaining than the dry tone I would have turned out on my own. I hope you enjoy the subtle humor.

I would not have taken the leap and started a business in the first place if it had not been for Scott Rupard, Tom Craddock and Bob Durr. They all owned their own businesses and inspired me to take the leap. They also freely discussed the good and bad of owning a business with me, and did much to dispel my fear of the unknown. Many of their key points are included in the book with examples from my own company.

Bill Gammerdinger was the dad at the Boy Scout campfire that started the discussion on what I would eventually call "Export Proof." He was also the one who suggested handing out $100 bills to recognize and motivate employees.

My brain trust — Patty Beach, Dale Brown, Kristin Bennett, Ellen Castro and from Sterling Partners, Mike Drai and Julie Stacey — has helped me for years in business. I called on them again for advice for this book. They had so many good suggestions that it took more than a year to incorporate them all.

A few others deserve special mention for their years of mentoring, and for being sounding boards for life in general. Bill McClung taught me a lot about how field techs think about their work and how important it is to recognize them for their skills and abilities. John Stolt, who talked me through many of the startup struggles at Desert from a rocking chair on the porch of Casa de Oro, is an All-Pro at business. Our different view points averaged out in conversation, and formed better solutions than either of us would have on our own. We both love the business of business, and never tire of discussing new ideas. Corey Jones, my son-in-law, has helped me grow by thinking about how to apply these business principles to service companies in general. I appreciate his willingness to share his experiences at the glass company for this book. His success with the glass company gave me confidence that the principles in this book have widespread application.

And of course, my friend and business partner, Don Bennett. He was my example of a successful small-business owner, and gave me something to shoot for after I was laid off. He discovered Desert was for sale, and told me about the opportunity in the first place. He also had a team ready to help me: Dan Hollman, my lawyer; James Riddle, my accountant; Guy Farmer, my banker; as well as Glen Elliott and Ronnie Williams, my insurance agents. That all-star team has provided me professional advice over the years that shows up throughout the book. Don believed in me and put his money, advice and coaching behind our fledgling service business. He's modest to say that our approach at Desert was nothing unique, but he's right: It's all about the execution.

Finally, I would like to acknowledge my wife, Allison. She has always believed in me and pushed me to find out about owning a small business. Without her, my story would have a completely different ending. From living on savings for years as we waited for the company to make a profit to the elation at the sale and the uncertainty of life afterwards, she has lived it all with me. I appreciate her willingness to share family stories about our values. She has been tolerant of my new writing hobby and has indulged me in the expense to have it published. Like me, she believes that we all have experiences to share that can help other people have better lives.

Index

www.ingramcontent.com/pod-product-compliance
Lightning Source LLC
Chambersburg PA
CBHW070539090426
42735CB00013B/3029